OFFICIAL SQA PAST PAPERS
WITH SQA ANSWERS

Higher
GEOGRAPHY

**Two Specimen Question Papers
and 2000 to 2002 Past Papers**

First exam published in 1999.

Published by
Leckie & Leckie Ltd, 8 Whitehill Terrace, St. Andrews, Scotland KY16 8RN
tel: 01334 475656 fax: 01334 47
hq@leckieandleckie.co.uk www.leckiea

Leckie & Leckie Project Team: Simon Appleford; Br
Cover Design Assistance: Mike Mi

ISBN 1-84372-052-3

A CIP Catalogue record for this book is available from the British Library.

Printed in Scotland by Inglis Allen on environmentally friendly paper. The paper is made
from a mixture of sawmill waste, forest thinnings and wood from sustainable forests.

® Leckie & Leckie is a registered trademark.

Leckie & Leckie

Introduction

The best way to prepare for exams is to practise, again and again, all that you have learned over the past year. Work through these questions and check your solutions against these *official SQA answers*. But give yourself a real chance and be honest! Make sure you work through each question thoroughly so that you understand how you got the right answer – *you will have to do this in the exam*!

Contents

Leckie & Leckie has made every effort to trace all copyright holders. If any have been inadvertently overlooked, Leckie & Leckie will be pleased to make the necessary arrangements. The following companies/individuals have very generously given permission to reproduce their copyright material free of charge:

Causeway Press Ltd for an extract from *Geography in Focus* by Ian Cook (p 105);
Nelson Thornes Ltd for an extract from *Themes & Issues – 1997 – National Parks in the UK* (p 102); an extract from *The Wider World* by David Waugh (p 31); and an extract from *Themes In Human Geography* by Mel Rockett (p 34);
Blackwell Publishers for an extract from AS Level Geography by A Bowen & J Pallister (p 110);
The Population Reference Bureau for a table (p 110);
The maps have been reproduced by kind permission of Ordnance Survey. © Crown Copyright NC/02/28038.

[C042/SQP017]

Higher
Geography

Time: 1 hour 25 minutes

NATIONAL
QUALIFICATIONS

Paper 1: Core
Revised Specimen Question Paper

Attempt all questions.

The value attached to each question is shown in the margin.

Credit will be given for appropriate models, diagrams, maps and graphs. Marks may be deducted for bad spelling, bad punctuation and for writing that is difficult to read.

Note The reference maps and diagrams in this paper have been printed in black only: no other colours have been used.

The map extract used is the 1:50 000 extract no 863/88: Sunderland

Copies may be obtained from the OS suppliers.

This is an updated version of the map extract used for the 1992 Geography Higher (Revised) Paper I.

SCOTTISH
QUALIFICATIONS
AUTHORITY
©

Extract No 863/88

1:50 000 Scale
Landranger Series

1 mile = 1· 6093 kilometres

Question 1 (Atmosphere)

Study Reference Diagram Q1.

Suggest both physical and human reasons for the variations in global temperature.

5

Reference Diagram Q1 (Global temperature change 1860–1990)

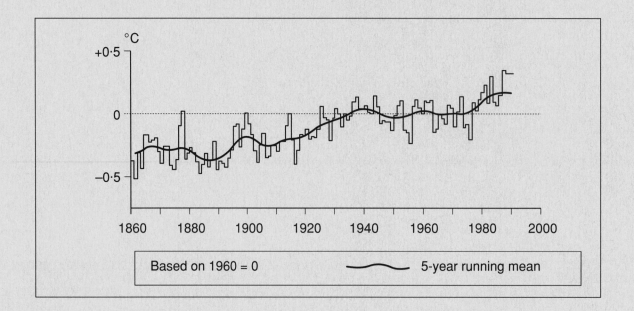

Question 2 (Hydrosphere)

Study OS map extract: Sunderland.

(*a*) Quoting map evidence, describe the **physical landscape of the River Wear and its valley** from GR 297472 to GR 284509.

3

(*b*) Choose any **one** of the **river features** you have described and, with the aid of a diagram or diagrams, explain its formation.

3

Question 3 (Lithosphere)

Study Reference Diagram Q3.

Explain how the features in **either** Area A **or** Area B have been formed.   **4**

Reference Diagram Q3 (A typical area of the Pennines)

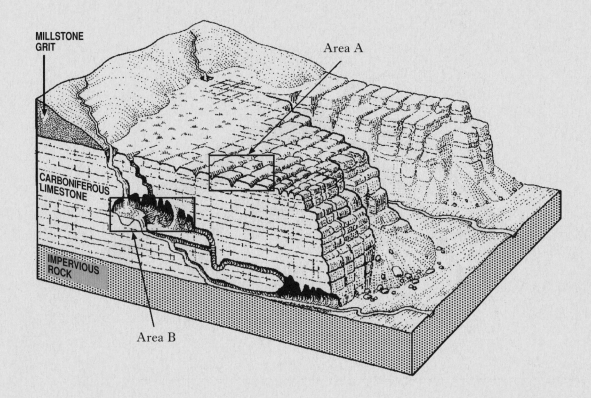

Question 4 (Biosphere)

Select **one** of the following soil types:
  (i)   podzol
  (ii)   brown earth
  (iii) gley.

With the aid of an annotated diagram of a soil profile, describe the soil forming processes that have contributed to its formation.   **5**

Question 5 (Population Geography)

Study Reference Map Q5.

(a) Describe in detail the pattern of migration shown on the map.   **3**

Reference Map Q5 (Migration to former West Germany, mid 1970s)

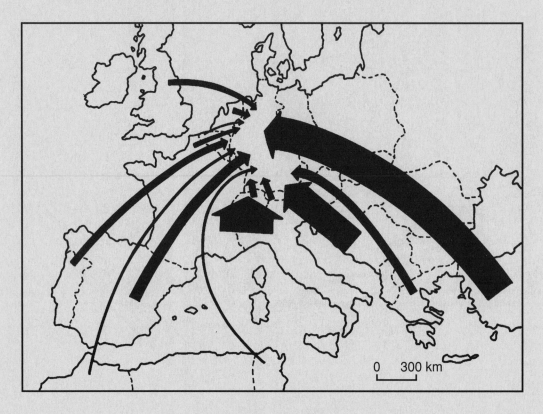

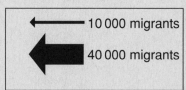

(b) *"Migrations such as those shown on the map are mostly the result of a combination of 'push' and 'pull' factors."*

Referring to any migration between two named countries, describe in detail

either the "push" factors

or the "pull" factors.   **3**

Question 6 (Rural Geography)

  (*a*) Describe the main characteristics of **shifting cultivation**.   **3**

  (*b*) Study Reference Diagram Q6.

      Referring to an area where shifting cultivation is practised, suggest possible reasons for fallow periods being reduced.   **3**

Reference Diagram Q6 (Relationship between soil productivity and length of fallow period in shifting cultivation)

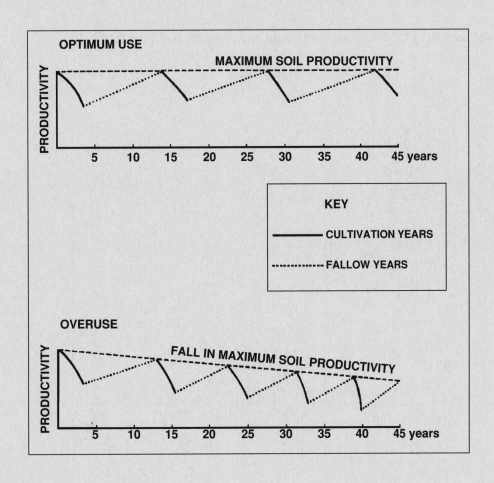

Question 7 (Industrial Geography)

Study Reference Map Q7.

With reference to a **named** industrial concentration in the European Union which you have studied, answer **either (a) or (b)**.

(a) Describe the **physical factors** which led to the growth of early industry.   4

OR

(b) Explain why **human and economic factors** have become more important in accounting for the location of industries today.   4

Reference Map Q7 (Selected industrial concentrations in the EU)

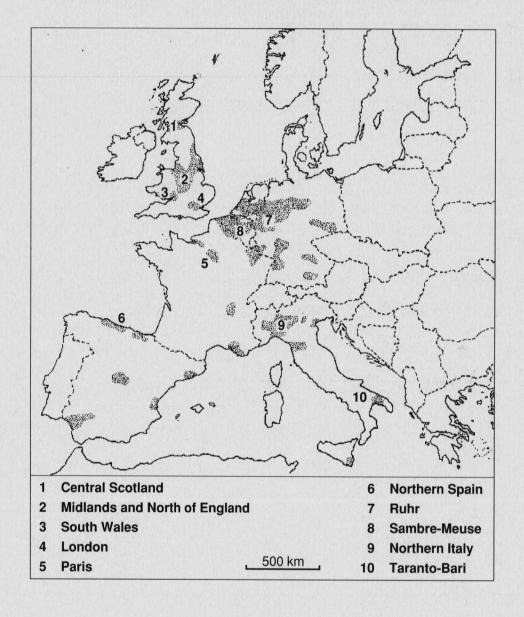

1	Central Scotland	6	Northern Spain
2	Midlands and North of England	7	Ruhr
3	South Wales	8	Sambre-Meuse
4	London	9	Northern Italy
5	Paris 500 km	10	Taranto-Bari

Question 8 (Urban Geography)

Marks

Study OS map extract: Sunderland and Reference Map Q8.

Choose **one** of the three urban zones marked (**A**, **B** and **C**) on Reference Map Q8 and,

(*a*) describe the features of the urban landscape, and

(*b*) suggest why this zone has developed at this particular location.

4

Reference Map Q8

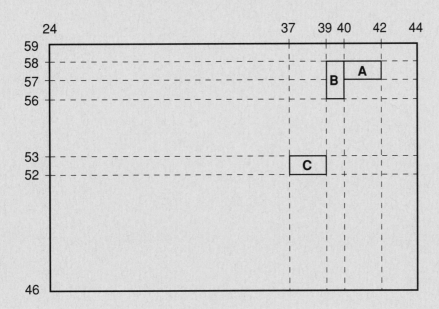

[END OF QUESTION PAPER]

[BLANK PAGE]

[C042/SQP017]

Higher	Time: 1 hour 20 minutes	NATIONAL
Geography		QUALIFICATIONS

Paper 2: Applications
Revised Specimen Question Paper

Two questions should be attempted.

One question from Section A (Questions 1, 2, 3) and
one question from Section B (Questions 4, 5, 6).

The value attached to each question is shown in the margin.

Credit will be given for appropriate models, diagrams, maps and graphs. Marks may be deducted for bad spelling, bad punctuation and for writing that is difficult to read.

Note The reference maps and diagrams in this paper have been printed in black only: no other colours have been used.

SCOTTISH
QUALIFICATIONS
AUTHORITY

SECTION A

You must answer ONE question from this Section

Question 1 (Rural Land Resources)   *Marks*

(*a*) Study Reference Diagram Q1.

   (i) Upland areas like Snowdonia contain glaciated features which make them attractive to visitors.

      Describe and explain the formation of such physical features in Snowdonia or in any glaciated upland area you have studied.   **9**

   (ii) With reference to Snowdonia or your chosen glaciated upland area, explain the social and economic opportunities created by a landscape such as this.   **7**

(*b*) For Snowdonia or any other upland area, describe environmental conflicts which have arisen and evaluate the effectiveness of solutions used to resolve these conflicts.   **9**

                                                          (25)

Reference Diagram Q1 (Landscape within Snowdonia National Park)

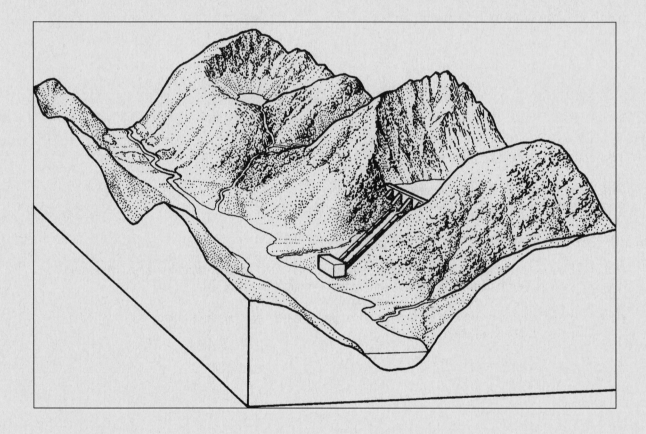

Question 2 (Rural Land Degradation)

Marks

(a)   Study Reference Diagram Q2.

Show how deforestation **and** inappropriate farming can contribute to the degradation of rural land.   **8**

(b)   For named areas in North America **and either** Africa north of the Equator **or** the Amazon basin, describe and explain the social and economic impact of land degradation on the people.   **7**

(c)   Referring to specific locations in North America,

   (i)   describe the methods used to try to reduce rural land degradation, and

   (ii)   evaluate the effectiveness of these methods.   **10**

(25)

Reference Diagram Q2 (Causes of land degradation)

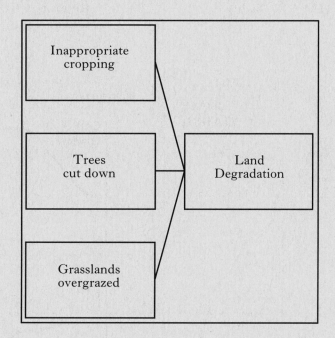

Question 3 (River Basin Management)

Marks

(a) Study Reference Map Q3 and Reference Diagram Q3.

With the aid of the resources, explain the need for water management in the Lower Nile Basin in Egypt.

4

(b) (i) With reference to a river basin you have studied in Africa **or** North America, explain the physical factors which have to be considered when selecting **sites** for dams and their associated reservoirs.

5

(ii) "*Water control projects not only bring social, economic, political and environmental benefits but also adverse consequences.*"

Referring to a river basin you have studied, evaluate the success of its water control projects in terms of their social, economic, political and environmental impact.

16

(25)

Reference Map Q3 (The Nile Basin)

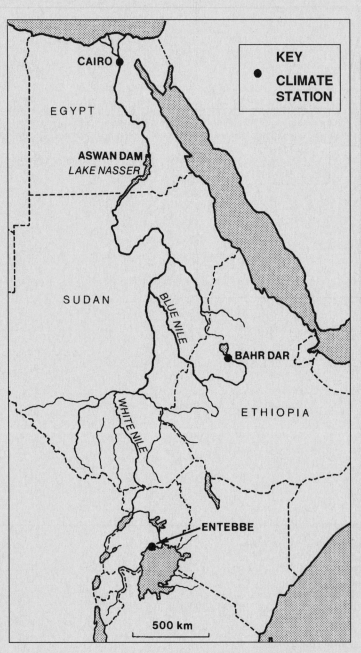

Reference Diagram Q3 (Selected climate graphs)

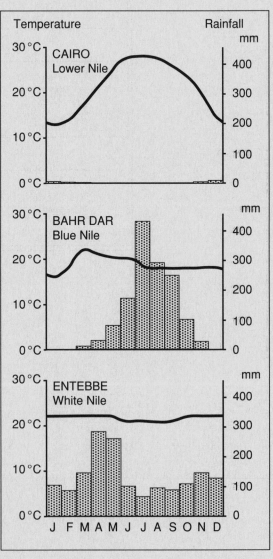

SECTION B

You must answer ONE question from this Section

Question 4 (Urban Change and its Management)   *Marks*

(*a*)   Study Reference Diagram Q4.

Major cities of the **Developed World** face a number of problems, eg poor quality housing, traffic congestion and industrial decline, as suggested in the diagram.

With reference to a named city you have studied in the Developed World, describe the ways in which such problems have been tackled, and evaluate the effectiveness of these solutions.   **15**

(*b*)   "Most cities in the **Developing World** are growing very rapidly."

With reference to a named city in the Developing World which you have studied, describe the social, economic and environmental problems created by its growth.   **10**

(25)

Question 4—continued

Reference Diagram Q4 (Managing urban change in a Developed World city 1950–2000)

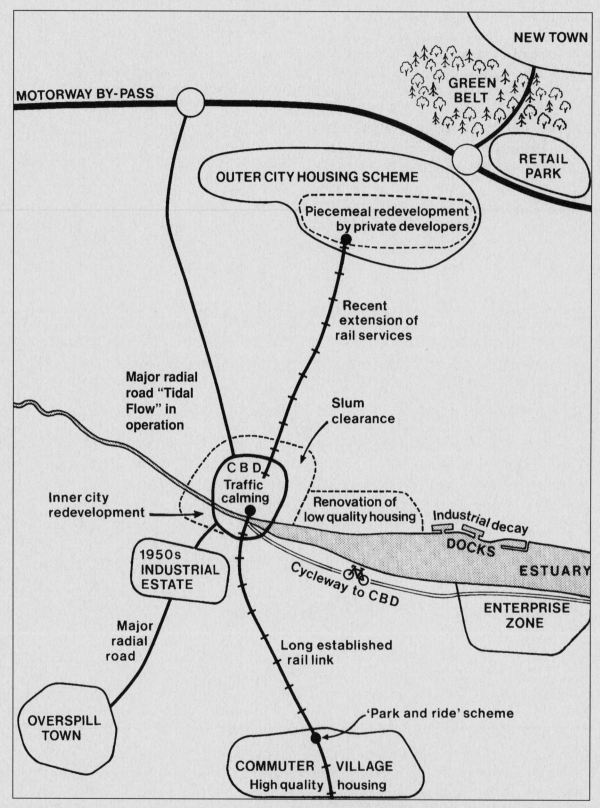

Not to scale

Question 5 (European Regional Inequalities)

Marks

(*a*)   Study Reference Map Q5.

Norte is one of the main industrial areas of Portugal, Lisbon is the capital city and Algarve is an important holiday region.

For each of these **three** regions, describe and explain the changing employment structure from 1950 to 1990.   **8**

(*b*)   For **either** Portugal **or** a **named** country you have studied in the European Union,

  (i)   describe and explain the physical and human factors which have led to regional inequalities, and   **9**

  (ii)   outline the steps taken by the national government and the European Union to assist the less prosperous regions, and assess the impact these steps have had on development.   **8**

(25)

Question 5—continued

Reference Map Q5 (Portugal: Regional Employment by sector)

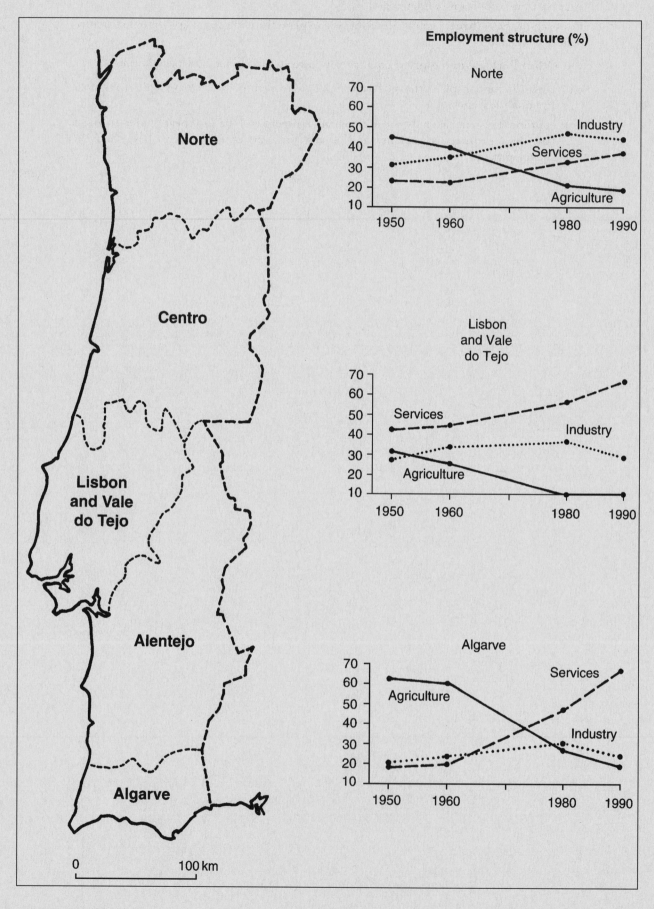

Question 6 (Development and Health)

Marks

(a) Study Reference Table Q6.

(i) Referring to the countries listed in the table **and/or** to other countries in the Developing World which you have studied, suggest reasons why such wide variations in development exist between countries.

6

(ii) Explain why such indicators of development may fail to provide an accurate representation of the true quality of life in a Developing Country.

5

(b) For **one** of the following diseases:

bilharzia (schistosomiasis)
or malaria
or cholera,

(i) describe the physical and human factors which put people at risk of contracting the disease,

(ii) describe the methods used to try to control the disease, commenting on their success,

(iii) explain how the prevention of the disease will benefit countries in the Developing World.

14

(25)

Reference Table Q6 (Indicators of development for selected countries)

Indicator (1995–97)	South Korea	Bangladesh	Brazil
GNP per capita (US Dollars)	9700	240	3640
Life Expectancy (years)	73	58	67
Birth Rate (per 1000)	15	31	22
Infant Mortality Rate (per 1000 live births)	11	77	48

[END OF QUESTION PAPER]

[BLANK PAGE]

X042/301

NATIONAL
QUALIFICATIONS

Time: 1 hour 30 minutes

GEOGRAPHY
HIGHER
Core
Additional Specimen
Question Paper

Attempt **all** questions.

The value attached to each question is shown in the margin.

Credit will be given for appropriate models, diagrams, maps and graphs.

Marks may be deducted for bad spelling, bad punctuation and for writing that is difficult to read.

Note   The reference maps and diagrams in this paper have been printed in black only: no other colours have been used.

SCOTTISH
QUALIFICATIONS
AUTHORITY
©

Extract No 1056/OLM2

1:25 000 Scale
Outdoor Leisure Series

Four colours should appear above; if not then please return to the invigilator.
Four colours should appear above; if not then please return to the invigilator.

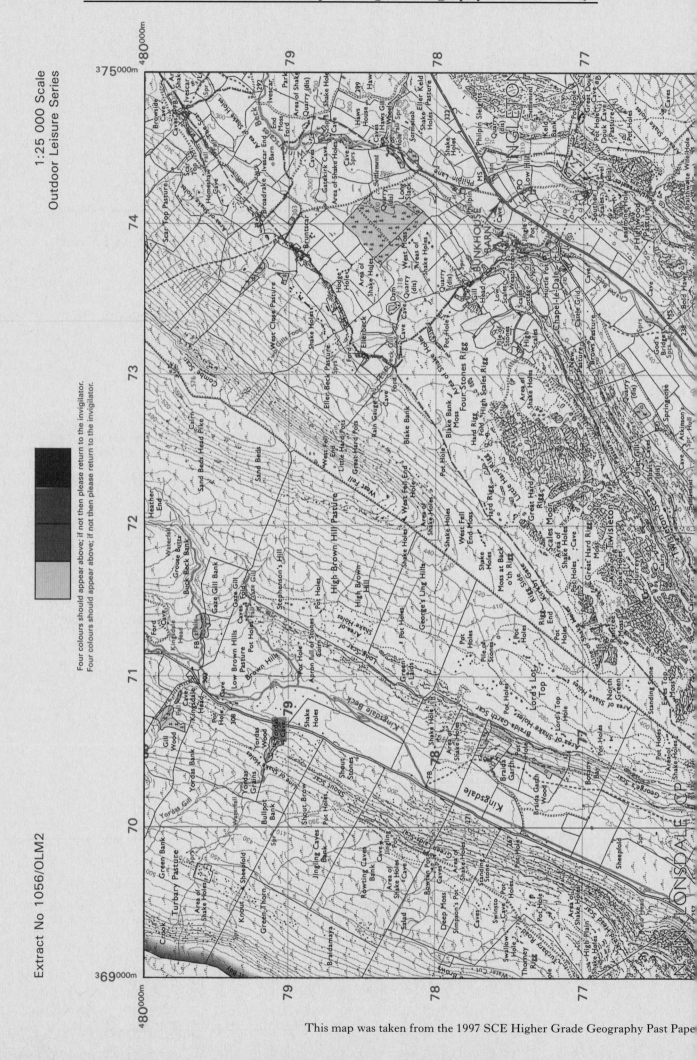

This map was taken from the 1997 SCE Higher Grade Geography Past Paper

Marks

Question 1

(*a*)   Study Reference Maps Q1A.

Describe the origin, nature and weather characteristics of **either** the Tropical Maritime **or** Tropical Continental air masses.

2

(*b*)   Study Reference Maps Q1A and Q1B.

Using the maps and graphs, **describe** and **explain** the pattern of annual rainfall in **either** Kano **or** Enugu.

4

Reference Maps Q1A (Location of selected air masses and the ITCZ in January and July)

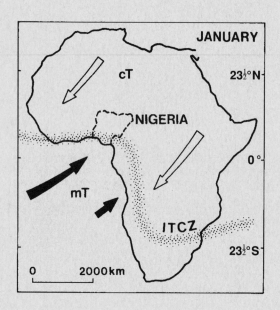 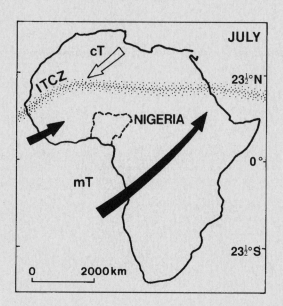

Question 1—continued

Reference Map Q1B (Length, in days, of the rainy season in Nigeria, and selected rainfall graphs)

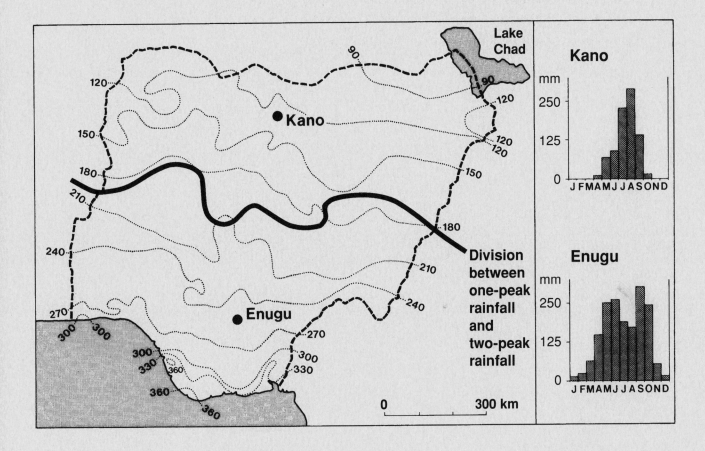

Marks

Question 2

Study OS map extract number 1056/OLM2: Ingleton (*separate item*).

Compare and **contrast** the physcal features of:

  (i)   the River Twiss and its valley from 694752 to 693731, and;

  (ii) the Kingsdale Beck and its valley from 709789 to 695763.

6

Marks

Question 3

Study OS map extract number 1056/OLM2: Ingleton (*separate item*).

The area of the Yorkshire Dales National Park, shown on the map, is characterised by Upland Limestone scenery.

Describe the evidence to support the above statement, referring to **specific named features** shown on the map extract.

6

Marks

Question 4

(*a*)   **Explain** fully what is meant by the term "climax vegetation".   **2**

(*b*)   **Describe** and **account for** the likely plant succession in
    either   (i)   a coastal dune belt
    or   (ii)   an area of derelict or abandoned land.
    Your answer should make reference to specific plants.   **5**

Marks

Question 5

Study Reference Diagram Q5.

For **either** a Developed Country (Diagram 5A) **or** a Developing Country (Diagram 5B), **describe** and **account for** the population structure shown.   6

Reference Diagram Q5 (Age Pyramids)

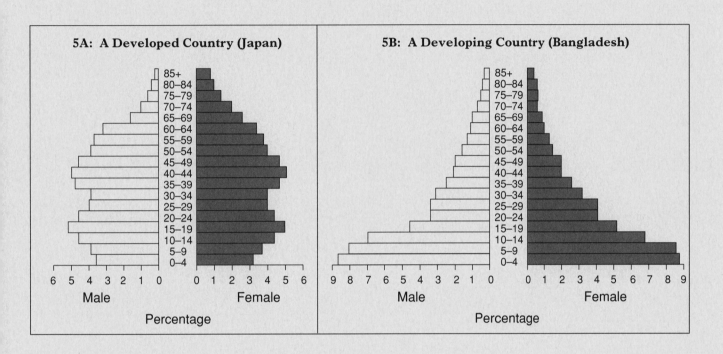

Marks

Question 6

Since 1950 many areas of intensive peasant farming have been changed due to the impact of the Green Revolution and many areas of shifting cultivation have been changed due to the impact of deforestation.

For **either** intensive peasant farming **or** shifting cultivation,

 (i) **describe** in detail the changes that have taken place, and

(ii) **assess** the impact these changes have had on the people, their ways of life and the landscape.

6

Marks

Question 7

Many industrial concentrations in Europe have experienced recent change.

(a) With reference to **one** named industrial concentration in the European Union, **describe** the **original** physical and human factors which led to the growth of industry.

3

(b) Study Reference Diagram Q7 which shows major developments in the former steel producing area around the Lower Don Valley at Sheffield.

Referring to the Lower Don Valley at Sheffield **or** any named industrial concentration in the European Union, **describe** the ways in which the **landscape** has changed as a result of redevelopment.

3

Reference Map Q7 (Planned developments in the Lower Don Valley, Sheffield)

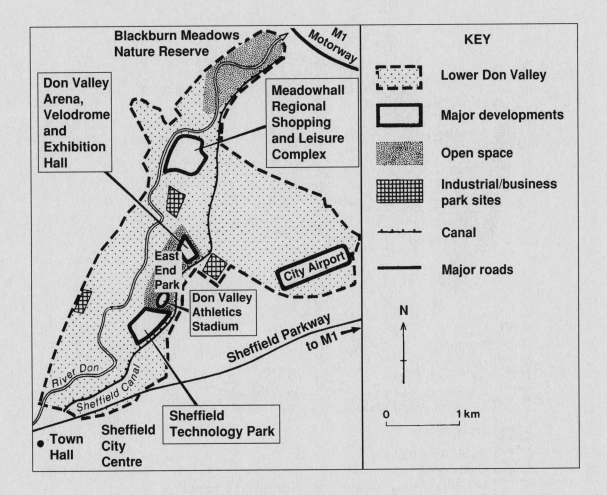

Marks

Question 8

(a) For any city you have studied in the Developed World, show how its original site and situation encouraged its growth.

3

(b) Study Reference Map Q8 which shows land use zones in Liverpool. Choose **one** of the land use zones **A or B** identified in the key.

Referring to Liverpool, **or** any other city you have studied in the Developed World, **describe** and **explain** the changes which have taken place in your chosen zone in recent years.

4

Reference Map Q8 (Land use zones in Liverpool)

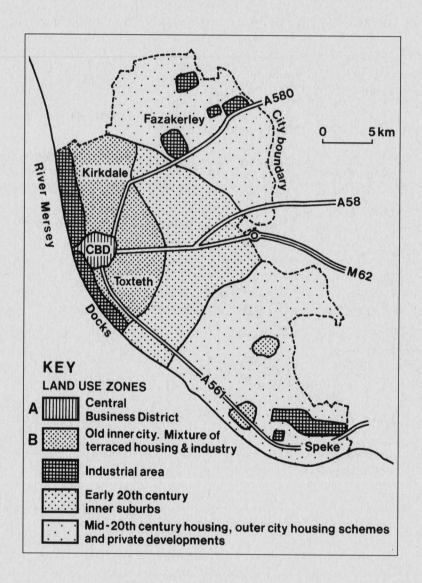

[END OF QUESTION PAPER]

X042/303

| NATIONAL QUALIFICATIONS | Time: 1 hour 15 minutes | **GEOGRAPHY** HIGHER Applications Additional Specimen Question Paper |

Two questions should be attempted.

One question from Section 1 (Questions 1, 2, 3) and
one question from Section 2 (Questions 4, 5, 6).

Write the numbers of the **two** questions you have attempted in the marks grid on the back cover of your answer booklet.

The value attached to each question is shown in the margin.

Credit will be given for appropriate models, diagrams, maps and graphs.

Marks may be deducted for bad spelling, bad punctuation and for writing that is difficult to read.

Note   The reference maps and diagrams in this paper have been printed in black only: no other colours have been used.

SCOTTISH QUALIFICATIONS AUTHORITY

Marks

SECTION 1

You must answer ONE question from this Section.

Question 1 (Rural Land Resources)

(*a*)   Study Reference Map Q1.

The Lake District is an area of outstanding glaciated upland scenery.

Describe and **explain** the formation of the glacial features in the Lake District **or** in any area of glaciated upland you have studied.   **12**

(*b*)   With reference to the Lake District **or** any glaciated upland you have studied, **explain** the social and economic opportunities created by the glaciated landscape.   **5**

(*c*)   *"The Lake District is a place of spectacular natural beauty. It is also a place of work, a home to 42 000 people and a tourist destination for over 12 million visitors every year."*

Describe and **explain** the environmental conflicts which may arise in areas like the Lake District where there is a concentration of visitors in certain locations.   **8**

     (25)

Reference Map Q1 (The Lake District)

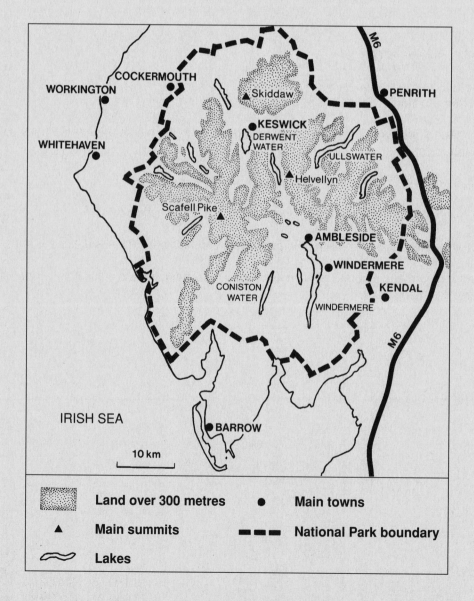

Marks

Question 2 (Rural Land Degradation)

(*a*)   Study Reference Diagram Q2.
        Explain the physical, social and economic causes of desertification.   **8**

(*b*)   For **either** the Amazon Basin **or** Africa north of the Equator, **describe** the
        environmental, social and economic consequences of rural land degradation.   **9**

(*c*)   Using examples from North America,

   (i)   **describe** and **explain** methods used to conserve soil resources, and

   (ii) **assess** how effective these conservation strategies have been.   **8**

                                                                                                  (25)

Reference Diagram Q2 (The cycle of desertification)

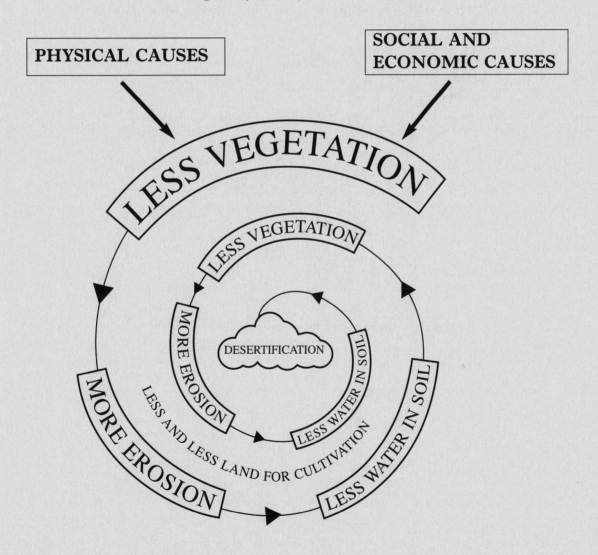

Marks

Question 3 (River Basin Management)

(*a*) Study Reference Map Q3 and Reference Diagrams Q3A and Q3B.

Explain why there is a need for water management in Northern Nigeria.   **5**

(*b*) For any river basin management scheme you have studied in North America **or** Africa:

(i) **explain** the **physical factors** which had to be considered when selecting sites for dams, and   **5**

(ii) **explain** how the scheme affects the hydrological cycle in the surrounding area.   **5**

(*c*) **Describe** and **account for** the social, economic and environmental benefits **and** adverse consequences of water control projects in a river basin you have studied.   **10**

(25)

Reference Map Q3 (Rainfall distribution in Nigeria and location of Sokoto Valley)

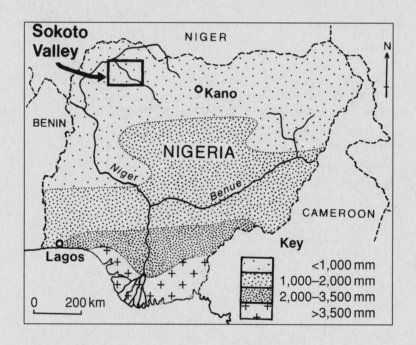

Question 3 – continued

Reference Diagram Q3A (Rainfall variability in the Sokoto Valley)

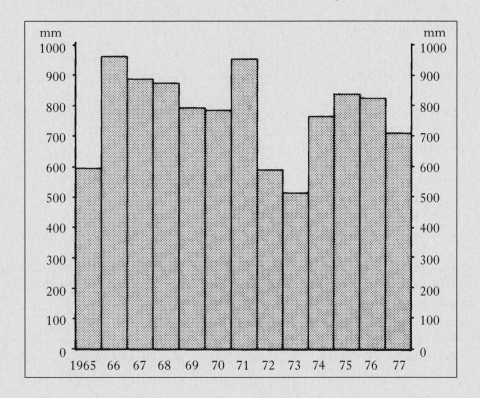

Reference Diagram Q3B (Mean monthly rainfall in the Sokoto Valley)

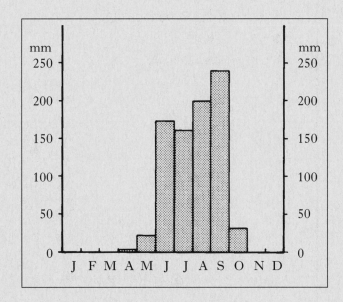

Marks

SECTION 2

You must answer ONE question from this Section.

Question 4 (Urban Change and its Management)

(*a*) Study Reference Diagram Q4, which gives information about Lagos, a typical city in the Developing World.

(i) **Describe** the changes in population growth, built-up area and population density in Lagos between 1890 and 1990.

(ii) **Comment** on the relationship between these indicators.   5

(*b*) For Lagos, **or** a named city you have studied in the **Developing** World:

(i) **describe** the economic, social and environmental problems which have resulted from the growth of the city, and

(ii) **describe** strategies employed by the city authorities to tackle these problems.   10

(*c*) "*There are many problems on the edges of cities in the **Developed** World, eg housing schemes in need of improvement and growing urban pressures on the rural-urban fringe.*"

For a **named** city you have studied in the **Developed** World:

(i) **outline** the factors which contribute to the problems found on the edges of cities, and

(ii) **describe** efforts made to solve these problems and **assess** how effective they have been.   10

          (25)

Reference Diagram Q4 (Lagos—population, area and density 1890–1990)

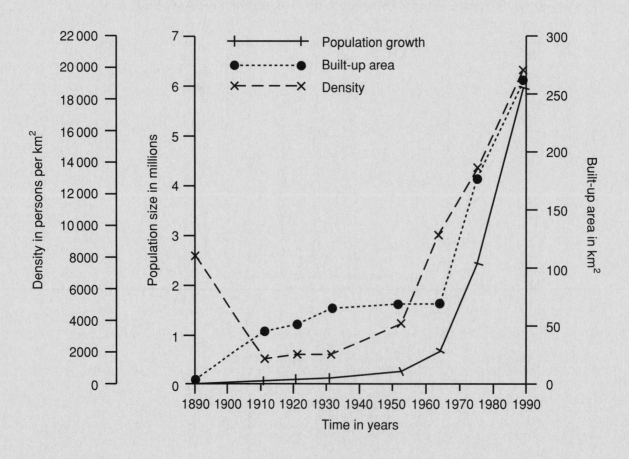

Marks

Question 5 (European Regional Inequalities)

(a)   Study Reference Map Q5A.

Suggest both physical **and** human reasons for the prosperity enjoyed within the area now
known as "Europe's Hot Banana".

6

(b)   Study Reference Map Q5B and Reference Table Q5.

Italy is often described as having a "North-South Divide". With reference to specific
provinces and data provided in the table, **comment** on the accuracy of this statement.

5

(c)   For Italy or any other country of the European Union which has marked differences in
economic development between regions, **describe** the physical **and** human factors which
have contributed to such regional differences.

7

(d)   For the country chosen in (c), **describe** the strategies used by both the national
government and the European Union to overcome these problems, and **comment** on their
effectiveness.

7

(25)

Reference Map Q5A (Europe's Hot Banana)

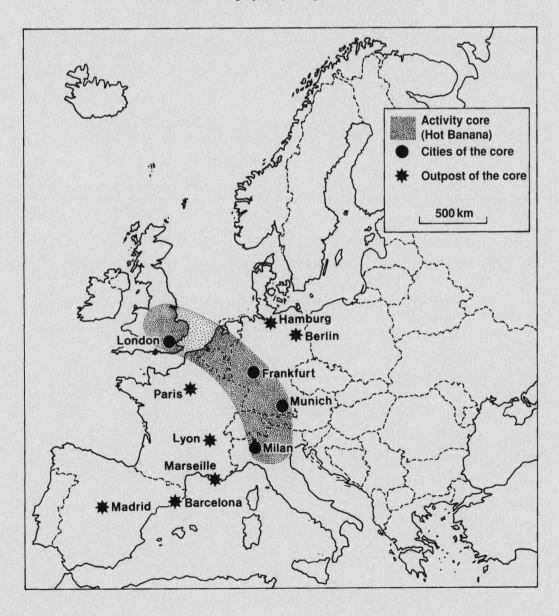

Question 5 – continued

Reference Map Q5B (Italy—GDP per capita, by provinces)

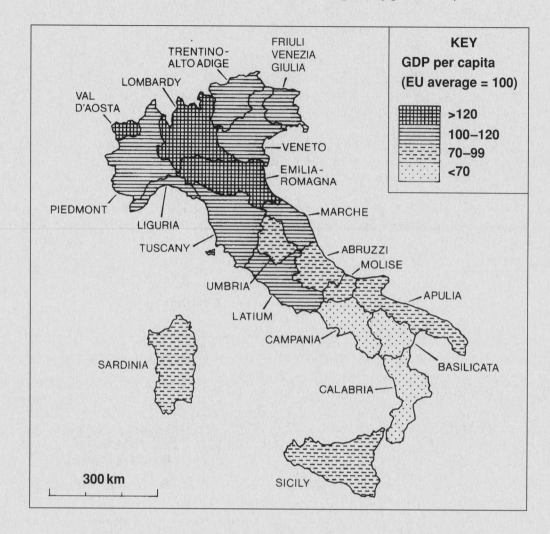

Reference Table Q5 (Italy—Percentage of total employment in selected sectors in North and South)

Employment sector	Percentage in north	Percentage in south
Industry	78	22
Commerce	65	35
Services	59	41

Marks

Question 6 (Development and Health)

(a)   Study Reference Map Q6, which shows the Physical Quality of Life Index (PQLI) for countries of the world.

    (i)   For **either** the PQLI **or** any similar composite measure of development, state **three** indicators which might be used in its calculation, and **comment** on the usefulness of the indicators.

        6

    (ii)   Referring to countries in the **Developing World** which you have studied, **suggest reasons** for variations **between** countries in their quality of life.

        5

    (iii)   **Explain** why indicators of development may not accurately reflect the quality of life **within** a country.

        4

(b)   For malaria, **or** bilharzia **or** cholera:

    (i)   **describe** the methods used to try to control the spread of the disease.

    (ii)   **comment** on how effective these methods of control have been.

        10

        (25)

Reference Map Q6 (Physical Quality of Life Index)

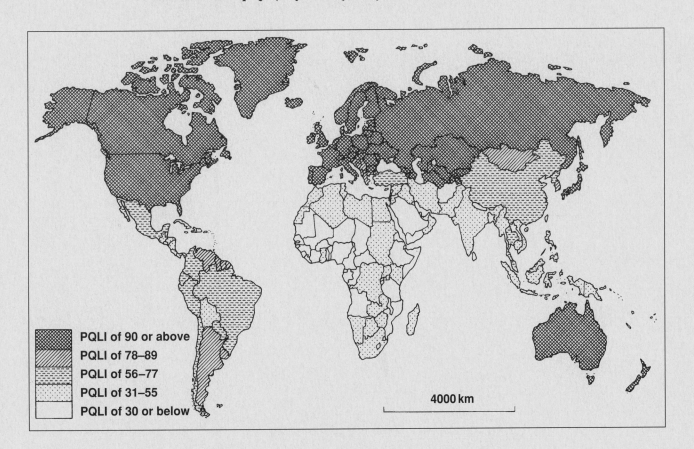

PQLI of 90 or above
PQLI of 78–89
PQLI of 56–77
PQLI of 31–55
PQLI of 30 or below

4000 km

[END OF QUESTION PAPER]

[BLANK PAGE]

X042/301

NATIONAL QUALIFICATIONS 2000	MONDAY, 5 JUNE 9.00 AM – 10.25 AM	GEOGRAPHY HIGHER Core

Attempt **all** questions.

The value attached to each question is shown in the margin.

Credit will be given for appropriate models, diagrams, maps and graphs.

Marks may be deducted for bad spelling, bad punctuation and for writing that is difficult to read.

Note   The reference maps and diagrams in this paper have been printed in black only: no other colours have been used.

SCOTTISH
QUALIFICATIONS
AUTHORITY

Extract No 1171/104

1:50 000 Scale
Landranger Series

1 mile = 1·6093 kilometres

Marks

Question 1

Study Reference Maps Q1 below and Reference Diagram Q1 opposite.

With the aid of the climate graph and the maps provided, describe and account for the climate of Jos in Central Nigeria.

5

Reference Maps Q1 (Selected air masses and fronts over Africa in January and July)

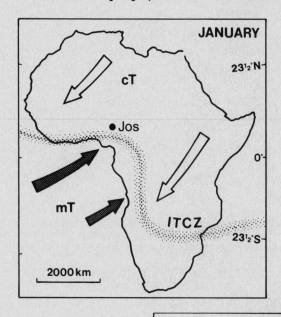 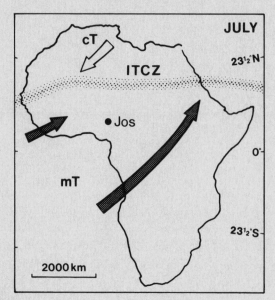

KEY

mT   **Tropical Maritime**

cT   **Tropical Continental**

ITCZ   **Inter Tropical Convergence Zone**

Question 1 – continued

Reference Diagram Q1 (Climate graph for Jos, Nigeria)

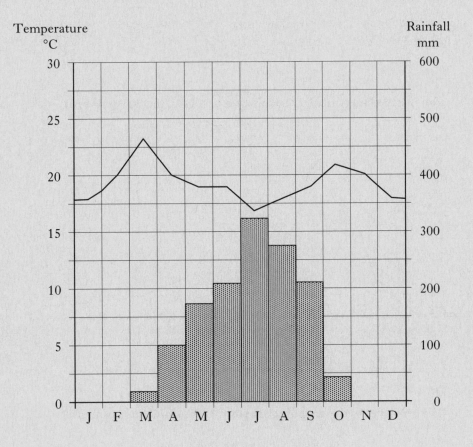

[Turn over

Marks

Question 2

Study Reference Diagram Q2.

Describe and account for the changes in discharge levels of the River Wyre between the 18th and the 19th of December 1993.

4

Reference Diagram Q2 (Discharge levels of the River Wyre)

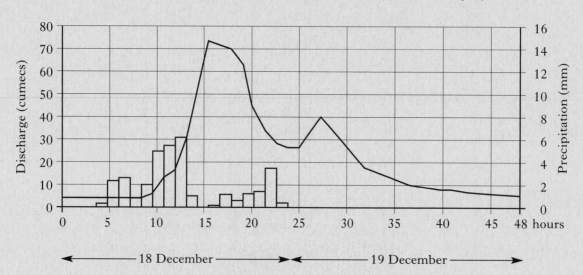

River Wyre: hydrograph at Scorton, 18th–19th December 1993

cumecs = cubic metres per second

Marks

Question 3

Study Reference Diagram Q3.

The landscape in the sketch contains features of both glacial erosion and glacial deposition.

Erosional features	Depositional features
Hanging valley	Drumlins
Corrie	Terminal moraine
Roche moutonnée	Esker

Select **one** feature of erosion and **one** feature of deposition, and explain the processes involved in the formation of each feature.

Annotated diagrams may be used.   **6**

Reference Diagram Q3 (A glaciated landscape)

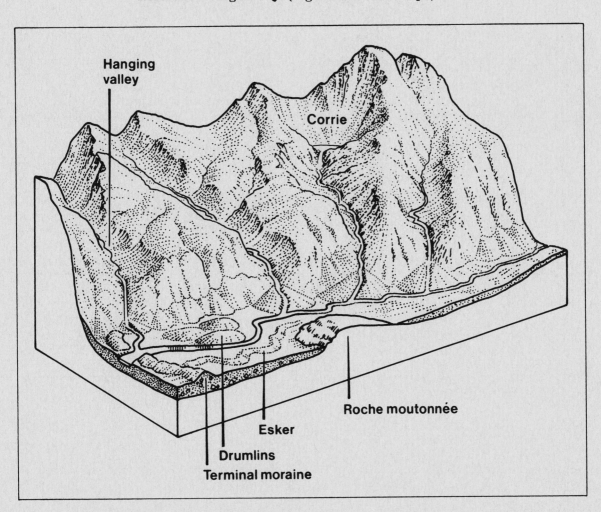

[**Turn over**

Marks

Question 4

The term *plant succession* describes the changes in vegetation that develop through time in a particular habitat.

Describe the process of plant succession, referring to

either

(*a*) a coastal sand dune area   **5**

or

(*b*) a derelict site.   **5**

Marks

Question 5

Study Reference Table Q5, which illustrates the projected ageing of the population within selected European Union countries.

Referring in your answer to **one** or **more** EU countries,

either

(*a*) suggest reasons for the population trend illustrated in the table   5

or

(*b*) discuss the likely consequences of the trend shown.   5

Reference Table Q5 (Ageing of the population within selected EU countries)

Persons 65+ as % of persons aged 15–64		
	1990	2040 (projected)
Belgium	21·9	41·5
Denmark	22·2	43·4
France	21·9	39·2
Germany	23·7	47·1
Greece	20·5	41·7
Ireland	18·4	27·2
Italy	20·4	48·4
Luxembourg	20·4	41·2
Netherlands	17·4	48·5
Portugal	16·4	38·9
Spain	17·0	41·7
UK	23·5	39·1
EU	**21·4**	**42·8**

[Turn over

Marks

Question 6

Choose **one** of the farming systems below and, referring to a named location, describe and explain the characteristics of the system.

(i)   Shifting cultivation

(ii) Intensive peasant farming

(iii) Extensive commercial farming   **4**

Marks

Question 7

Study OS map extract number 1171/104: Leeds (*separate item*) and Reference Map Q7.

(*a*)   Using map evidence, explain why manufacturing industry grew up in Area A in the nineteenth century.   3

(*b*)   Study Reference Table Q7.

"*Changes in employment figures for Leeds are similar to those of many old industrial areas of Western Europe.*"

For **either** Leeds **or** any other industrial concentration in the European Union you have studied, explain why these changes in employment have taken place.   3

Reference Map Q7

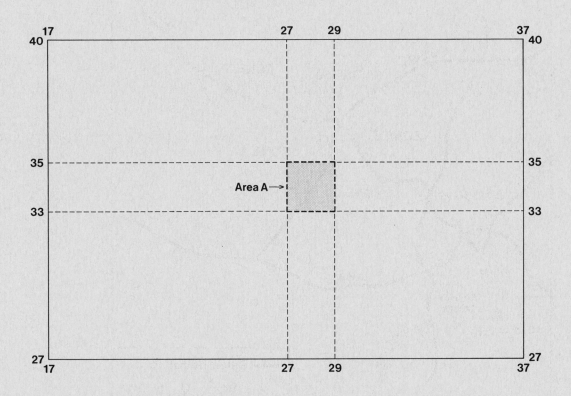

Reference Table Q7 (Employment in Leeds 1949 and 1998)

Employment sector	1949	1998
Manufacturing	148 328	55 800
Construction	14 395	13 000
Distribution	32 104	75 800
Transport and communications	17 969	18 300
Finance and business	5460	69 000
Public administration	8389	79 800

Marks

Question 8

Study OS map extract number 1171/104: Leeds (*separate item*) and Reference Map Q8.

(a) Suggest the likely function of Zone 1, giving map evidence to support your answer.   **2**

(b) Zones 2 and 3 show contrasting housing areas.

For **either** Zone 2 **or** Zone 3, describe the likely environment.   **3**

Reference Map Q8

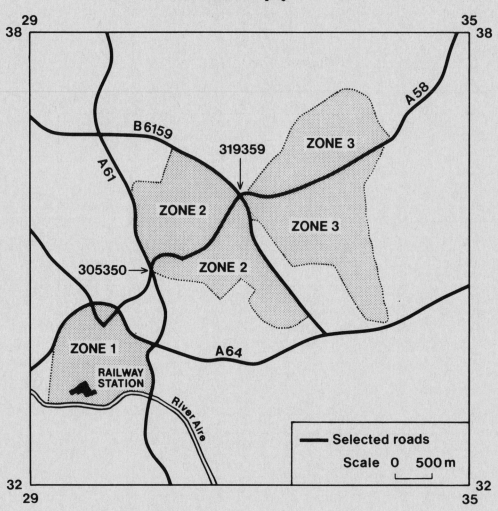

[*END OF QUESTION PAPER*]

X042/303

| NATIONAL QUALIFICATIONS 2000 | MONDAY, 5 JUNE 10.45 AM – 12.05 PM | GEOGRAPHY HIGHER Applications |

Two questions should be attempted.

One question from Section 1 (Questions 1, 2, 3) and
one question from Section 2 (Questions 4, 5, 6).

Write the numbers of the **two** questions you have attempted in the marks grid on the back cover of your answer booklet.

The value attached to each question is shown in the margin.

Credit will be given for appropriate models, diagrams, maps and graphs.

Marks may be deducted for bad spelling, bad punctuation and for writing that is difficult to read.

Note   The reference maps and diagrams in this paper have been printed in black only: no other colours have been used.

SCOTTISH
QUALIFICATIONS
AUTHORITY

Marks

SECTION 1

You must answer ONE question from this Section.

Question 1 (Rural Land Resources)

(a)   Study Reference Diagram Q1.

Describe **and** explain fully the structure, relief and drainage of the upland and lowland areas shown on the diagram.   **10**

(b)   *"Upland areas in the UK have become areas where land use conflicts have occurred."*

For any **named** upland area in the UK,

   (i)   outline the main conflicts which have taken place,

   (ii)   explain the opposing points of view, and

   (iii)   suggest ways in which conflicts can be resolved.   **10**

(c)   *"Various measures are now used to control agricultural production."*

For **either** Set Aside **or** Quotas,

   (i)   describe the main aims of the scheme, and

   (ii)   comment on its effectiveness.   **5**

     (25)

Reference Diagram Q1 (A scarp and vale landscape in England)

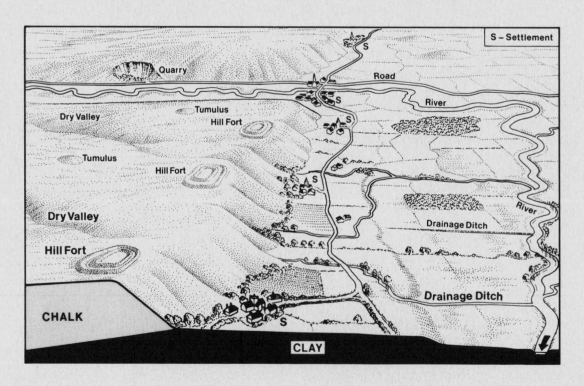

Marks

Question 2 (Rural Land Degradation)

(a) Study Reference Diagram Q2.

For **either** Africa north of the Equator, **or** the Amazon Basin,

(i) explain the ways in which natural processes and human activities contribute to the degradation of rural land,   **10**

(ii) describe the social and economic impact of land degradation on the population.   **7**

(b) With reference to specific locations in North America,

(i) describe the methods used to combat rural land degradation, and

(ii) assess the effectiveness of the methods employed.   **8**

(25)

Reference Diagram Q2 (Processes in land degradation)

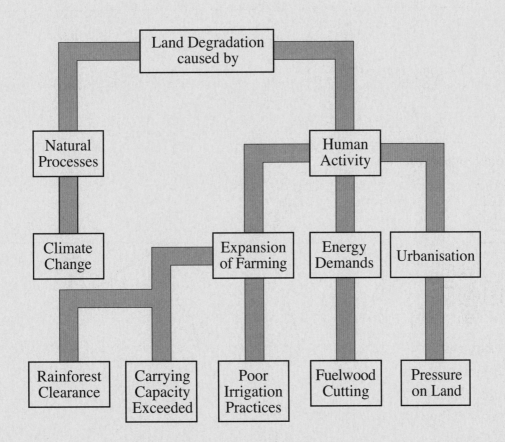

[Turn over

Marks

Question 3 (River Basin Management)

(a) *"Multi-purpose water projects are multi-million pound investments for countries."*
Study Reference Diagram Q3 and suggest reasons why such projects are so expensive.   **5**

(b) Explain the ways in which water control projects may change the hydrological cycle of a river basin.   **5**

(c) Explain the physical factors that have to be considered when selecting sites for dams and their associated reservoirs.   **5**

(d) For any river basin you have studied in **either** Africa **or** North America, discuss the social, economic and environmental benefits and adverse consequences of water control projects.   **10**

    (25)

Reference Diagram Q3 (A managed river basin)

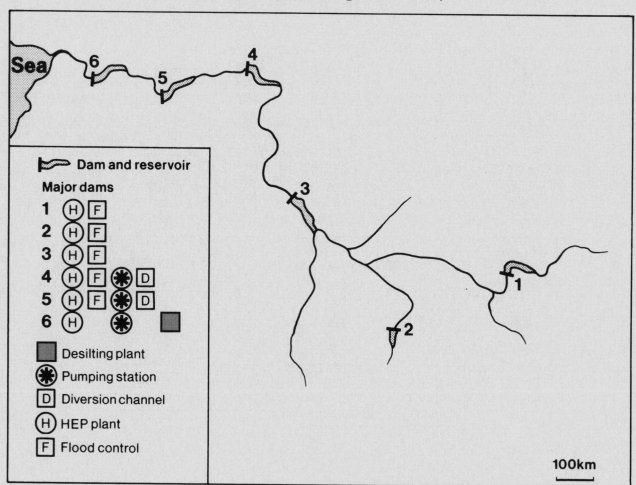

[SECTION 2 begins on *Page six*

[Turn over

Marks

SECTION 2

You must answer ONE question from this Section.

Question 4 (Urban Change and its Management)

(*a*)   Study Reference Map Q4A.

Describe and suggest reasons for the distribution of major cities in France **or** in another **Developed** Country you have studied.   **5**

(*b*)   Study Reference Map Q4B opposite.

    (i)   With reference to Paris **or** another city you have studied in the **Developed** World, describe the plans for its development and the strategies to deal with its problem areas. (Your answer may include changes in housing, employment and infrastructure.)

    (ii)   Assess how effective these plans and strategies have been.   **10**

(*c*)   With reference to a city you have studied in the **Developing** World,

    (i)   describe and account for its rapid growth, and

    (ii)   identify the social and economic problems which have resulted from its rapid growth.   **10**

    (25)

Reference Map Q4A (Major cities of France)

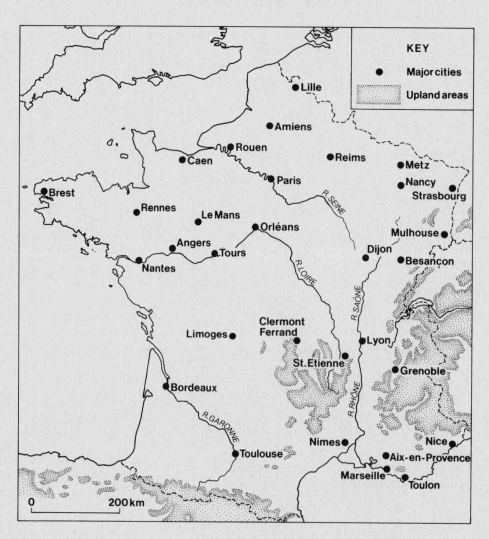

Question 4 – continued

Reference Map Q4B (Paris: Development Plan)

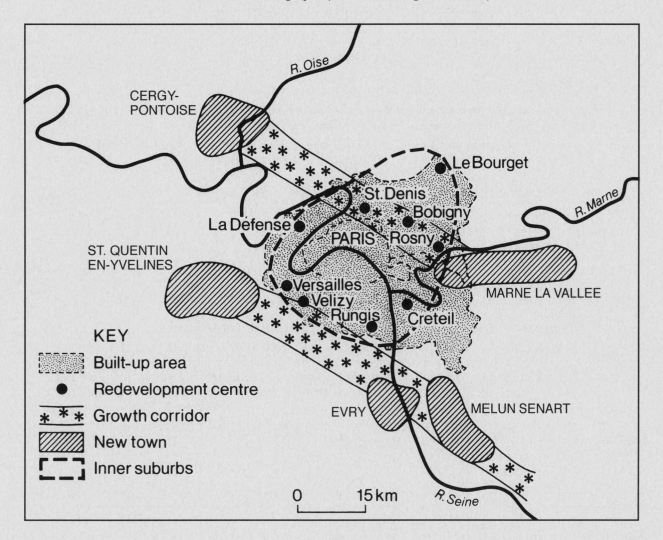

KEY

- ▨ Built-up area
- ● Redevelopment centre
- ✳ ✳ ✳ Growth corridor
- ▨ New town
- ⌐ ¬ Inner suburbs

0   15 km

[Turn over

Marks

Question 5 (European Regional Inequalities)

"Levels of wealth and economic development are not evenly spread within individual countries."

(a) Study Reference Table Q5 below and Reference Map Q5 opposite.
Suggest ways in which Italy illustrates the above statement.   5

(b) For Italy, **or** any other country in the European Union (EU),

  (i) describe the human and physical factors which have contributed to regional differences in wealth and economic development, and

  (ii) outline some of the social and economic problems which can result from these differences.   12

(c) For the country chosen in (b),

  (i) describe the steps which have been taken by the national government and the EU to overcome these problems, and

  (ii) comment on their effectiveness.   8

                     (25)

Reference Table Q5 (Italy – selected indicators of development)

	Birth rate per 1000 (1993)	Migration (% 1993)	Unemployment (% April 1994)	% under 15 (1993)	% over 65 (1993)	GNP per person (ECU 1993)
Italy average	**10·1**	**3·0**	**11·4**	**15·8**	**15·4**	**100**
North-West	7·6	4·4	8·9	12·1	18·6	115
Lombardy	8·7	4·0	6·1	13·8	14·6	130
North-East	9·0	3·9	6·3	14·0	16·0	115
Emilia-Romagna	7·2	7·2	6·6	11·4	19·6	124
Central	7·8	5·0	7·9	12·9	19·3	104
Lazio	10·0	2·9	11·0	15·3	14·2	115
Abruzzi-Molise	10·1	4·4	11·3	16·5	17·1	87
Campania	14·6	0·4	23·1	21·5	11·2	68
South	12·6	−1·0	17·5	20·3	12·9	67
Sicily	13·8	1·6	21·9	20·0	13·8	68
Sardinia	9·8	1·4	20·3	18·3	12·6	75

Question 5 – continued

Reference Map Q5 (Italy – Regions)

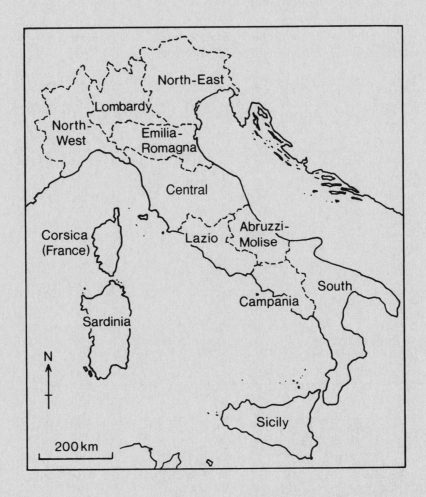

[Turn over

Marks

Question 6 (Development and Health)

(*a*) Study Reference Map Q6 below, which shows levels of development in Africa, using a "combined" indicator, the Human Development Index.

  (i) Suggest **one** social and **one** economic indicator of development and show how each might illustrate a country's level of development.   4

  (ii) Explain why indicators of development may fail to provide an accurate representation of the true quality of life **within** a country.   5

  (iii) Suggest reasons why variations in levels of development occur **between** countries in the Developing World.   4

(*b*) Study Reference Diagram Q6 opposite, which shows the main causes of child deaths in the Developing World.

  (i) Describe some of the steps which are being taken to reduce the occurrence of these health problems in Developing countries.

  (You may refer in your answer to specific disease control measures and/or to general health care measures.)

  (ii) Comment on how effective these steps have been.   12

(25)

Reference Map Q6 (Africa – Human Development Index)

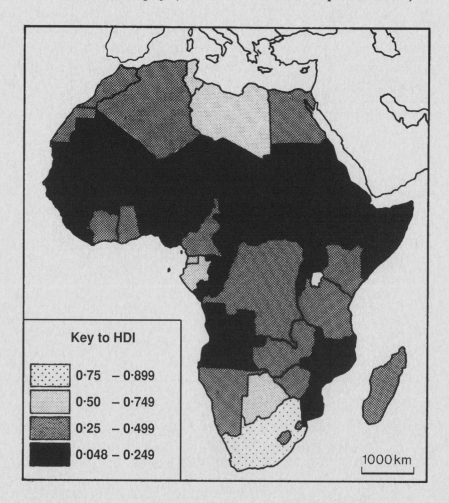

Key to HDI

0·75 – 0·899

0·50 – 0·749

0·25 – 0·499

0·048 – 0·249

1000 km

Question 6 – continued

Reference Diagram Q6 (Main causes of death, annually, of children under 5 in the Developing World)

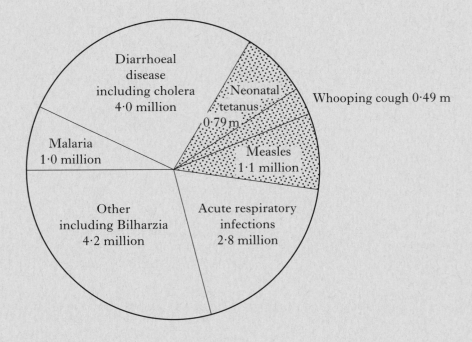

Vaccine preventable disease

[END OF QUESTION PAPER]

[BLANK PAGE]

X042/301

NATIONAL QUALIFICATIONS 2001	WEDNESDAY, 23 MAY 9.00 AM – 10.25 AM	**GEOGRAPHY** HIGHER Core

Attempt **all** questions.

The value attached to each question is shown in the margin.

Credit will be given for appropriate models, diagrams, maps and graphs.

Marks may be deducted for bad spelling, bad punctuation and for writing that is difficult to read.

Note   The reference maps and diagrams in this paper have been printed in black only: no other colours have been used.

SCOTTISH
QUALIFICATIONS
AUTHORITY

Extract No 1216/124

Four colours should appea
Four colours should appea

Scale

2 centimetres to

1 kilometre = 0·6214 mile

Grid North

Magnetic North   True North

Diagrammatic only

1:50 000 Scale
Landranger Series

Marks

Question 1

Study Reference Diagram Q1.

Suggest **physical** and **human** factors which might have contributed to the variations in temperature shown in Reference Diagram Q1.

5

Reference Diagram Q1 (Variations in average world temperatures 1850–1990)

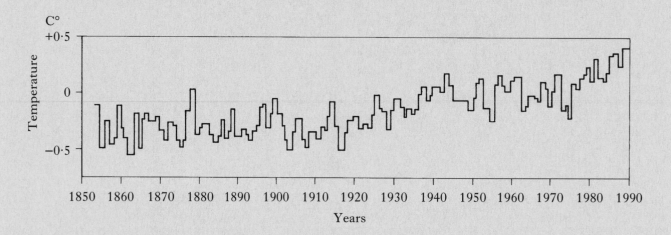

Marks

Question 2

Study OS map extract number 1216/124: Dolgellau (*separate item*).

Using appropriate grid references, **describe** the **physical characteristics** of the Afon (River) Dysynni and its valley from 710094 to 608050 (where it "leaves" the map extract).   **4**

Question 3

Study OS map extract number 1216/124: Dolgellau (*separate item*), and Reference Map Q3.

(*a*) The area within Area A, shown on Reference Map Q3, has been greatly affected by glacial erosion.

Identify **two** different features of glacial erosion in this part of the map extract, and give their grid references.   **2**

(*b*) Choose **one** of these features of glacial erosion and, with the aid of annotated diagrams, **explain** how it was formed.   **4**

Reference Map Q3

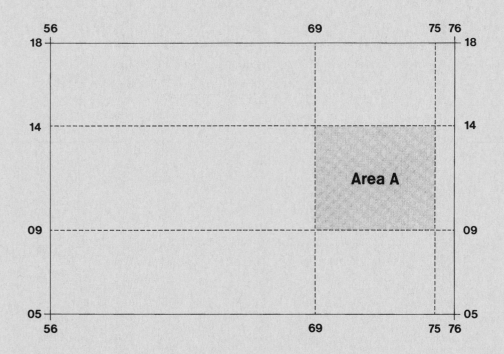

[Turn over

Marks

Question 4

Study Reference Diagram Q4 which shows information collected from a field survey of a coastal sand dune transect.

Suggest reasons for the changes in vegetation along the line of the transect. You should refer to a range of environmental factors.

5

Reference Diagram Q4 (Main plant types along a coastal sand dune transect)

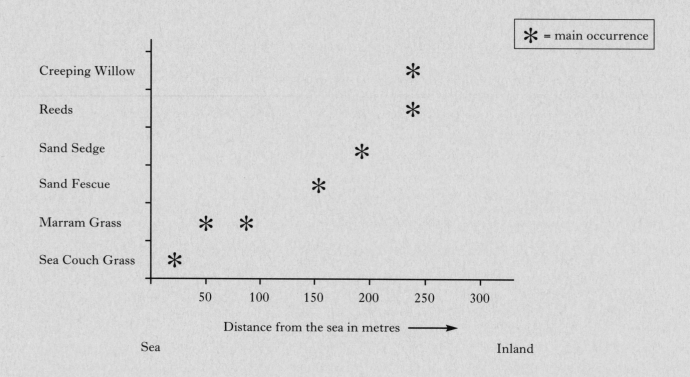

Marks

Question 5

Study Reference Diagram Q5.

India has a population structure which is typical of that of many **Developing** Countries.
Describe and **account for** the population structure shown.   5

Reference Diagram Q5 (India: population pyramid 1991)

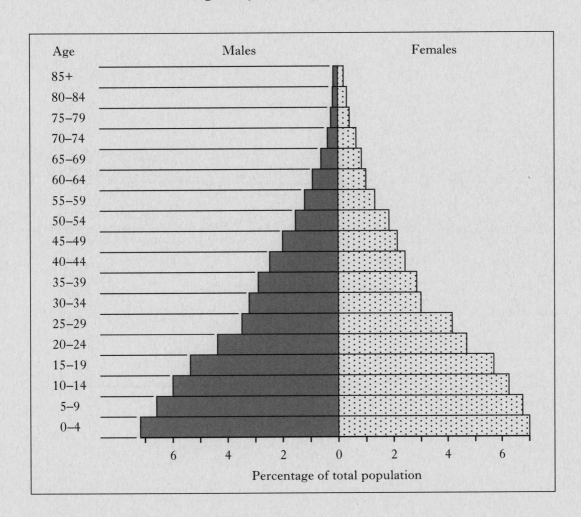

[Turn over

Marks

Question 6

Study Reference Diagram Q6.

For this area, or any area of intensive peasant farming you have studied, **describe** and **account for** the main features of the farming landscape.

5

Reference Diagram Q6 (An intensive peasant farming landscape in Southern Asia)

Marks

Question 7

Study Reference Diagram Q7.

With reference to **one named** industrial concentration in the European Union which you have studied, **explain** how such factors **originally** attracted industry to your chosen area.

5

Reference Diagram Q7 (Factors affecting the location of industry)

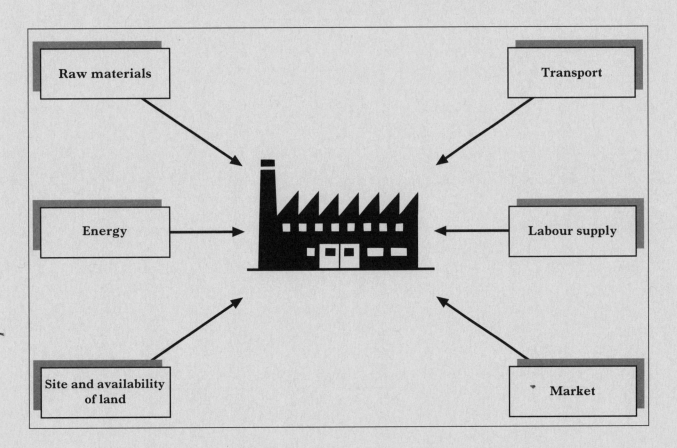

[Turn over for Question 8 on *Page eight*

Marks

Question 8

"*The Central Business District of major cities undergoes continuing change.*"

Referring to a city that you have studied in the **Developed** World, **explain** the changes which have taken place in the CBD over the past few decades.

You should refer to named locations within the CBD.   **5**

[END OF QUESTION PAPER]

X042/303

| NATIONAL QUALIFICATIONS 2001 | WEDNESDAY, 23 MAY 10.45 AM – 12.05 PM | GEOGRAPHY HIGHER Applications |

Two questions should be attempted.

One question from Section 1 (Questions 1, 2, 3) and
one question from Section 2 (Questions 4, 5, 6).

Write the numbers of the **two** questions you have attempted in the marks grid on the back cover of your answer booklet.

The value attached to each question is shown in the margin.

Credit will be given for appropriate models, diagrams, maps and graphs.

Marks may be deducted for bad spelling, bad punctuation and for writing that is difficult to read.

Note   The reference maps and diagrams in this paper have been printed in black only: no other colours have been used.

SCOTTISH
QUALIFICATIONS
AUTHORITY

Marks

SECTION 1

You must answer ONE question from this Section.

Question 1 (Rural Land Resources)

(*a*) Study Reference Map Q1.

Upland areas of the UK include areas of **Carboniferous Limestone** landscape and Chalk and Jurassic Limestone uplands characterised by their **Scarp and Vale** landscape.

Choose **one** of these types of landscape and, with the aid of annotated diagrams, **explain** how the main features of the physical landscape were formed.   **10**

(*b*) For any **named** upland area of the UK which you have studied, **explain** the main social and economic opportunities provided by the landscape.   **6**

(*c*) For your chosen upland area,

(i)   **give examples** of environmental conflicts which have arisen, and

(ii) **describe** some of the measures taken to resolve these conflicts and **comment** on their effectiveness.   **9**

                                                                                                (25)

Reference Map Q1 (Chalk and Limestone upland areas in England)

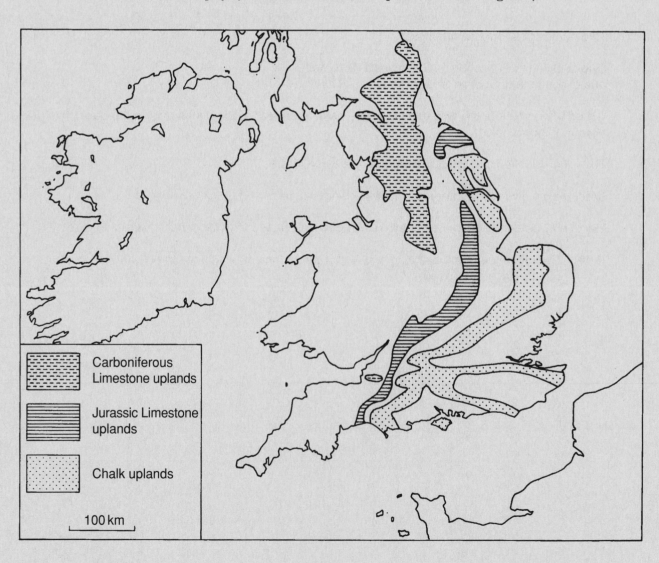

Marks

Question 2 (Rural Land Degradation)

(*a*) Study Reference Diagram Q2.

Describe in detail the **physical factors** which have led to land degradation in named areas of North America **and either** Africa North of the Equator **or** the Amazon Basin.   **7**

(*b*) Referring to named locations in **either** Africa North of the Equator **or** the Amazon Basin, **describe** the social, economic and environmental impact of rural land degradation.   **9**

(*c*) Referring to named areas of North America, **describe** the measures which have been taken to try to conserve soil and reduce land degradation, and **comment** on their effectiveness.   **9**

(25)

Reference Diagram Q2 (Physical factors which can lead to land degradation)

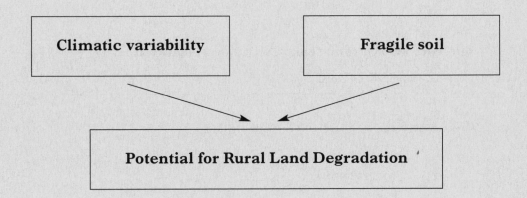

[Turn over

Marks

Question 3 (River Basin Management)

(*a*)   Study Reference Map Q3 and Reference Diagram Q3A which show the location of dams in the Tennessee Valley Authority.

With reference to the Tennessee Valley **or** any other river basin you have studied in North America **or** Africa, **explain** the **human and physical factors** that have to be considered when selecting sites for dams and their associated reservoirs.   **7**

(*b*)   Study Reference Diagram Q3B.

With reference to your chosen river basin, **explain** how water management projects have affected the hydrological cycle of the river basin.   **5**

(*c*)   For your chosen river basin, **explain**

    (i)   why there was a need for a water management project, and

    (ii)   the benefits which were gained from the water management project.   **13**

    (25)

Reference Map Q3 (The Tennessee Valley Authority area)

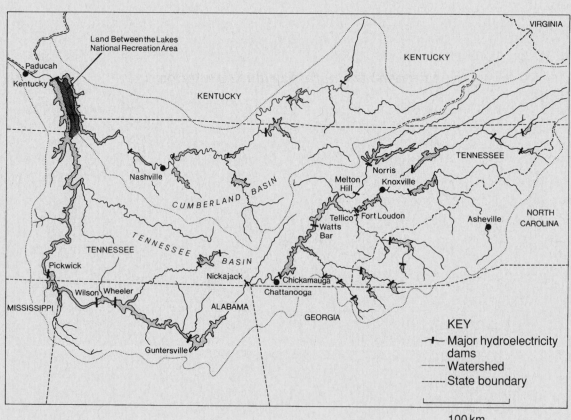

Question 3 – continued

Reference Diagram Q3A (Location of major dams on the Tennessee River)

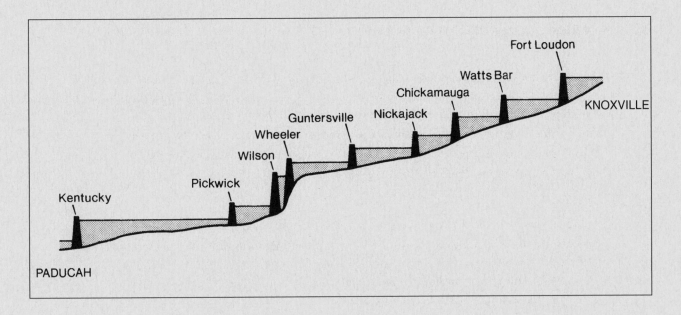

Reference Diagram Q3B (The hydrological cycle)

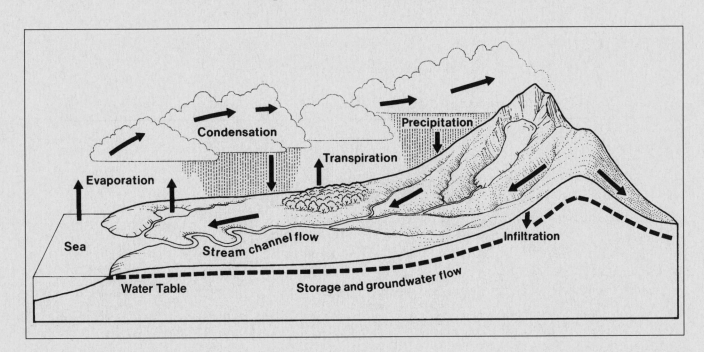

[Turn over

Marks

SECTION 2

You must answer ONE question from this Section.

Question 4 (Urban Change and its Management)

(a) Study Reference Diagram Q4 which highlights the problem of urban sprawl, faced by many countries in the Developed World.

With reference to a **named** city in the **Developed** World,

    (i)   **describe** some of the problems caused by the continued expansion of the city,

    (ii)   **describe** strategies which have been introduced to halt the spread of the city, and

    (iii)   **comment** on the effectiveness of these strategies.   **10**

(b) Study Reference Map Q4.

"Delhi has shanties scattered across the city rather than restricted to the periphery."

For Delhi, **or** a **named** city you have studied in the **Developing** World, **describe** the factors which have

    (i)   led to the growth of shanty towns, and

    (ii)   influenced the location of shanty towns.   **8**

(c) *"Many cities in the Developing World are taking steps to improve the quality of life for their residents."*

With reference to the city you have chosen in (b), **describe** the schemes designed to improve the quality of life in the city, and **comment** on their effectiveness.   **7**

                                                      (25)

Reference Diagram Q4 (Urban sprawl)

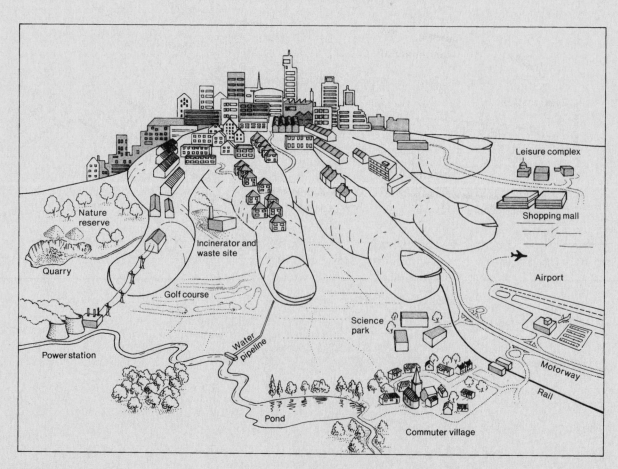

Question 4 – continued

Reference Map Q4 (Distribution of shanties in Delhi)

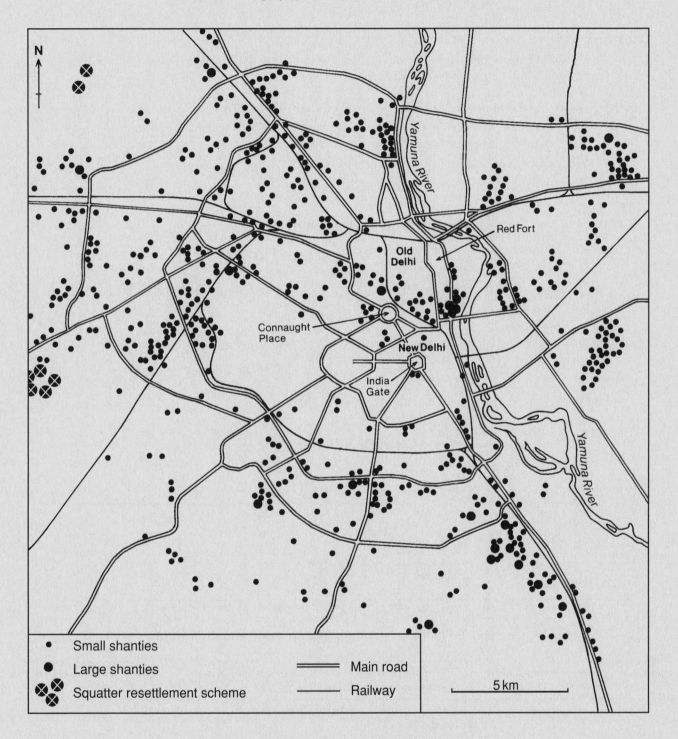

[Turn over

Marks

Question 5 (European Regional Inequalities)

(*a*)   Study Reference Map Q5 and Reference Table Q5.

In what ways does the data provide evidence of regional inequalities within Spain?   **5**

(*b*)   For **either** Spain **or** a named country you have studied in the European Union, **describe** and **explain** both the physical **and** human factors which have led to regional inequalities.   **10**

(*c*)   For **either** Spain **or** a named country you have studied in the European Union,

(i)   **describe** the steps taken by the national government and the European Union to tackle problems in the less prosperous regions, and

(ii)   **comment** on the effectiveness of these steps.   **10**

          (25)

Reference Map Q5 (Spanish Regions)

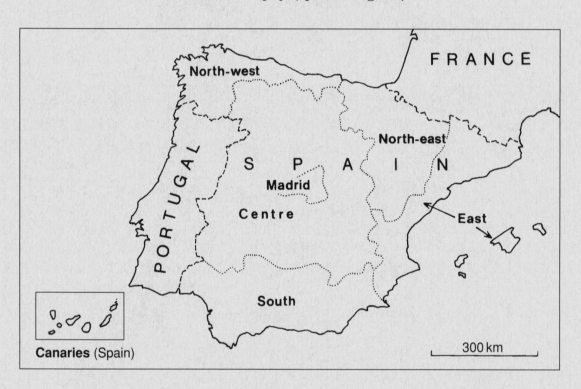

Reference Table Q5 (Socio-economic data for the regions of Spain)

Region	Area (% of total)	Population (% of total)	Percentage of Population		Employment % in			Unemployment Rate (%)	GDP per head (EU = 100)
			Aged under 15	Aged 65 and over	Agriculture	Industry	Services		
Spain			16·9	15·1	8·6	29·4	62·0	22·3	77
North-west	8·9	10·5	14·7	17·8	21·4	27·2	51·4	20·4	65
North-east	14·0	9·7	14·2	16·5	6·4	35·1	58·5	17·9	91
Madrid	1·6	15·0	16·3	13·3	1·0	26·0	73·0	20·6	96
Centre	42·6	13·0	16·5	18·4	14·3	29·4	56·3	22·2	65
East	11·9	26·0	16·2	15·3	4·6	34·9	60·5	19·4	89
South	19·6	22·1	20·3	12·7	10·9	22·9	66·2	31·3	59
Canaries	1·4	3·7	19·6	10·4	8·3	19·2	72·5	21·7	75

Marks

Question 6 (Development and Health)

(a) Study Reference Table Q6.

  (i) **Suggest reasons** for the differences in development between Newly Industrialising Countries and other Developing Countries. You should refer in your answer to Newly Industrialising Countries and Developing Countries you have studied. **6**

  (ii) **Explain** why indicators of development such as those used in Reference Table Q6 may fail to reflect accurately the true quality of life **throughout** a country. **4**

(b) Study Reference Map Q6 which shows the main areas of the world at risk from cholera.

  Referring to cholera, **or** malaria, **or** bilharzia/schistosomiasis,

  (i) **describe** the physical **and** human factors which put people at risk of contracting the disease,

  (ii) **describe** and **evaluate** the strategies used in controlling the spread of the disease, and

  (iii) **explain** the benefits to Developing Countries of controlling the disease. **15**

  (25)

Reference Table Q6 (Indicators of development for two countries)

Indicators	Sample Newly Industrialising Country South Korea	Sample Developing Country Sudan
People per doctor	1176	11 364
Life expectancy (years)	70	50
GDP per capita (US$)	4081	467

Reference Map Q6 (Countries with recent cholera outbreak)

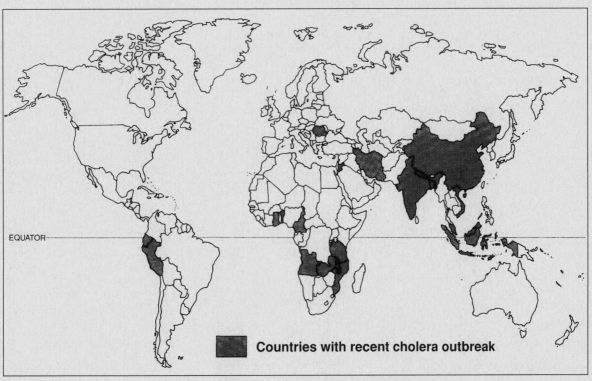

EQUATOR

■ **Countries with recent cholera outbreak**

[END OF QUESTION PAPER]

[BLANK PAGE]

X042/301

NATIONAL   WEDNESDAY, 5 JUNE   GEOGRAPHY
QUALIFICATIONS   9.00 AM – 10.30 AM   HIGHER
2002   Core

Attempt **all** questions.

The value attached to each question is shown in the margin.

Credit will be given for appropriate models, diagrams, maps and graphs.

Marks may be deducted for bad spelling, bad punctuation and for writing that is difficult to read.

Note   The reference maps and diagrams in this paper have been printed in black only: no other colours have been used.

SCOTTISH
QUALIFICATIONS
AUTHORITY

1:50 000 Scale
Landranger Series

Four colours should appear
Four colours should appear

Grid North

Magnetic North

True North

Diagrammatic only

Scale

2 centimetres

1 kilometre = 0·6214 mile

Extract No 1269/171

1 mile = 1·6093 kilometres

Marks

Question 1

Study Reference Diagram Q1.

(*a*) **Describe** the latitudinal variation of the Earth's energy balance shown in the diagram.   **2**

(*b*) With the aid of an annotated diagram of the Earth, **explain** the variations.   **4**

Reference Diagram Q1 (Latitude and energy balance)

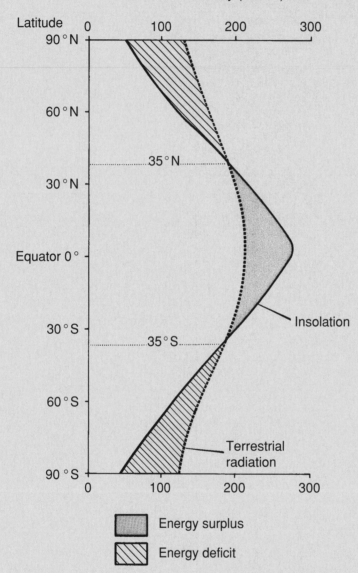

Marks

Question 2

Study Reference Diagram Q2 and Reference Maps Q2.

(*a*) **Describe** the variations throughout the year in the flow of the river Niger at Mopti.   2

(*b*) Using the diagram and the maps, **suggest reasons** for the variations in the flow.   4

Reference Diagram Q2 (Hydrograph and precipitation—River Niger at Mopti)

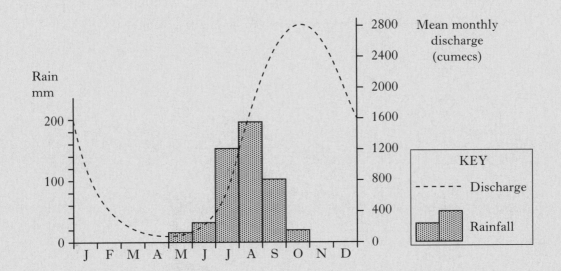

Reference Maps Q2 (Selected air masses and fronts over Africa in January and July)

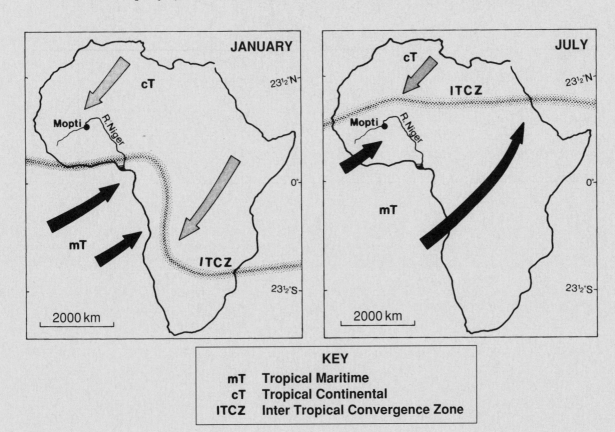

KEY

mT **Tropical Maritime**
cT **Tropical Continental**
ITCZ **Inter Tropical Convergence Zone**

Marks

Question 3

Study Reference Diagram Q3.

Select **two** features from the following list and **explain** the processes involved in their formation:

  (i)   limestone pavement;

  (ii) gorge;

  (iii) stalactites and stalagmites.

7

Reference Diagram Q3 (Carboniferous Limestone landscape)

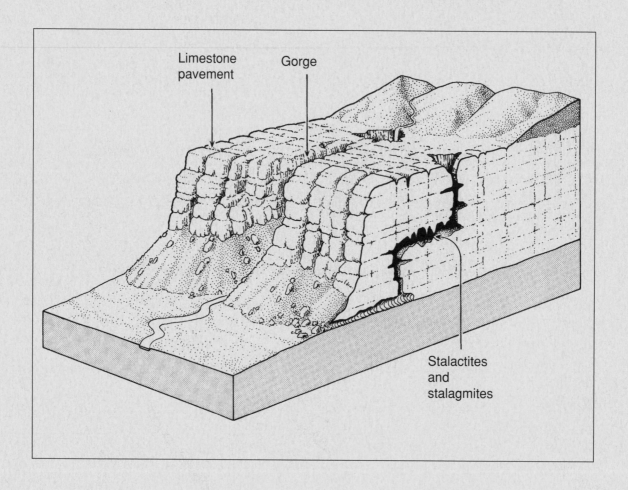

Marks

Question 4

Study Reference Diagram Q4.

Select **one** of the following soil types:

(i)   gley;

(ii) podzol;

(iii) brown earth.

With the aid of an annotated sketch of a soil profile, **explain how** the major soil forming
factors shown in the diagram have contributed to its formation.

6

Reference Diagram Q4 (Main factors affecting soil formation)

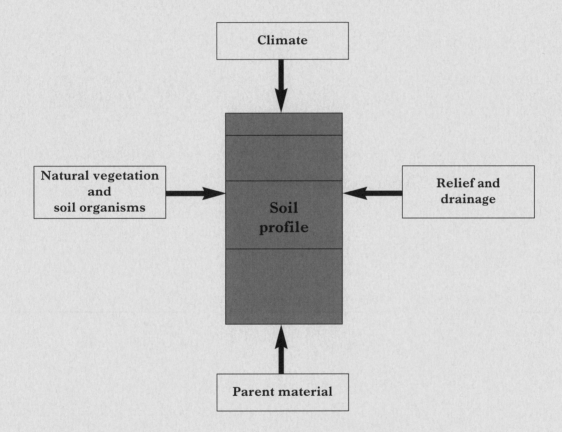

[Turn over

Marks

Question 5

Study Reference Diagram Q5.

International migrations may be **voluntary** or **forced**.

Referring to **one named** example of **each** type of migration, **explain** why the migration took place.

6

Reference Diagram Q5 (A model of migration)

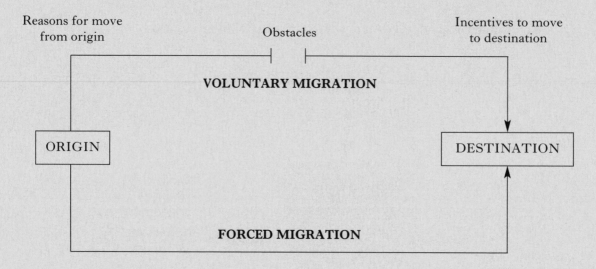

Marks

Question 6

Study Reference Diagram Q6 which shows the relative importance of the elements of shifting cultivation.

"Shifting cultivation remains an important farming system in many Tropical areas."

For a named location, **describe** and **explain** the characteristics of this farming system.   **6**

Reference Diagram Q6 (Elements of the system of shifting cultivation)

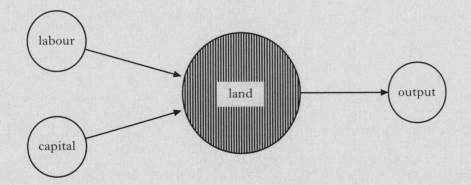

[Turn over

Marks

Question 7

Study OS map extract number 1269/171: Cardiff (*separate item*), and Reference Map Q7.

Using map evidence, **describe** and **explain** the physical and human factors which encouraged industry to locate in Area A.

6

Reference Map Q7

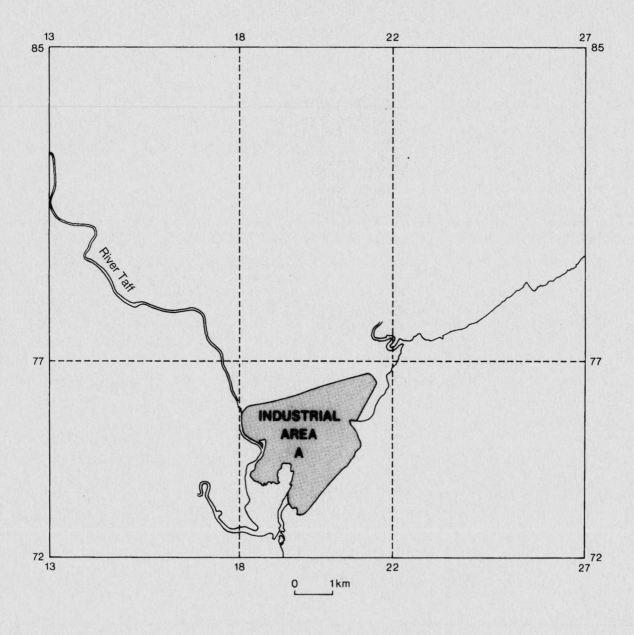

Marks

Question 8

Study OS map extract number 1269/171: Cardiff (*separate item*), and Reference Map Q8.

Describe the urban environments of Areas X and Y and **suggest reasons** for the differences.   **7**

Reference Map Q8

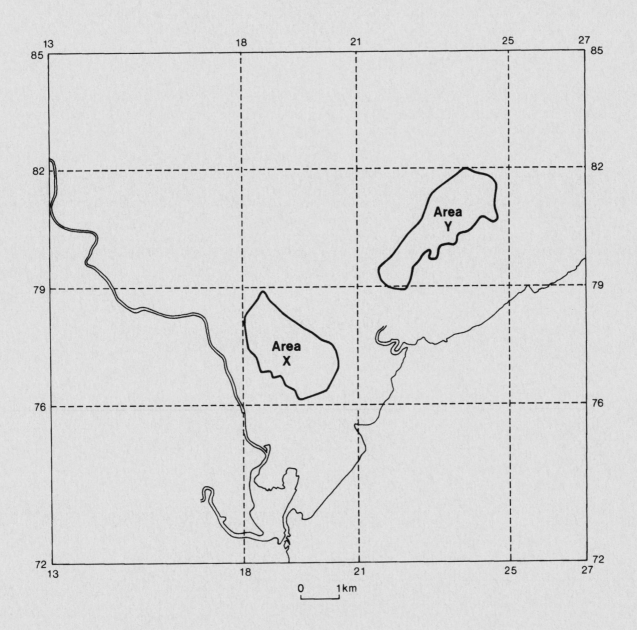

[END OF QUESTION PAPER]

[BLANK PAGE]

X042/303

NATIONAL
QUALIFICATIONS
2002

WEDNESDAY, 5 JUNE
10.50 AM – 12.05 PM

GEOGRAPHY
HIGHER
Applications

Two questions should be attempted.

One question from Section 1 (Questions 1, 2, 3) and
one question from Section 2 (Questions 4, 5, 6).

Write the numbers of the **two** questions you have attempted in the marks grid on the back cover of your answer booklet.

The value attached to each question is shown in the margin.

Credit will be given for appropriate models, diagrams, maps and graphs.

Marks may be deducted for bad spelling, bad punctuation and for writing that is difficult to read.

Note   The reference maps and diagrams in this paper have been printed in black only: no other colours have been used.

SCOTTISH
QUALIFICATIONS
AUTHORITY

Marks

SECTION 1

You must answer ONE question from this Section.

Question 1 (Rural Land Resources)

(a)   Study Reference Map Q1.

Suggest why different National Parks attract widely differing numbers of visitors.   **5**

(b)   *"Large numbers of visitors to a National Park can create environmental problems for those who live there."*

Referring to locations in a named National Park or upland area in the UK which you have studied:

    (i)   **give examples** of environmental problems which result from high numbers of visitors;

    (ii)   **describe** how such problems are tackled, and

    (iii)   **comment** on the effectiveness of these measures.   **10**

(c)   The Lake District and Snowdonia are particularly noted for their glaciated scenery.

For **either** of these National Parks **or** another named glaciated upland area in the UK, **explain**, with the aid of annotated diagrams, how the main features of the physical landscape were formed.   **10**

Reference Map Q1 (National Parks, visitor numbers, and main centres of population)   **(25)**

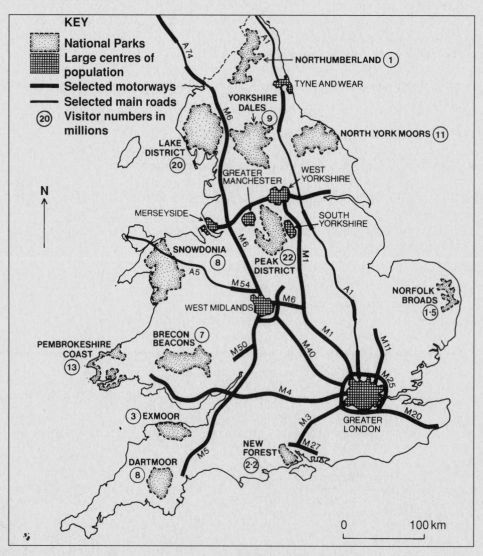

Marks

Question 2 (Rural Land Degradation)

"The rain clouds dropped a little spattering and hurried on to some other country. In the dust there were drop craters where the rain had fallen, and there were clean splashes on the corn and that was all."

(John Steinbeck)

(*a*) **Describe** the physical **and** human causes of land degradation in North America.   **8**

(*b*) **Explain** the impact of land degradation on the people and environment of:

    (i)   North America, **and**

    (ii) **either** Africa north of the Equator **or** the Amazon Basin.   **10**

(*c*) **Describe** the solutions which have been employed to control land degradation in **either** Africa north of the Equator **or** the Amazon Basin. **Comment** on the effectiveness of these methods.   **7**

(25)

[Turn over

Marks

Question 3 (River Basin Management)

(*a*) Study Reference Map Q3, Reference Diagram Q3A and Reference Diagram Q3B. Reference Diagram Q3B shows the variation in the discharge of the River Nile before and after the Aswan High Dam was built in 1963.

    (i) **Describe** and **account for** the pattern of river flow **before** the dam was built.

    (ii) **Describe** the ways in which the river's flow has changed since the completion of the dam.   **7**

(*b*) **Describe** and **account for** the social, economic and environmental benefits **and** adverse consequences of water control projects in a river basin you have studied in **either** Africa **or** North America.   **13**

(*c*) "*The next war in our region will be over the waters of the Nile.*"

                   Dr Boutros Boutros-Ghali, Egyptian, former UN Secretary-General

For a river basin you have studied,

    (i) **explain** the political problems which have resulted, or may result, from the building of multi-purpose water projects, and

    (ii) **suggest** how these problems may be resolved.   **5**

                                                   (25)

Reference Map Q3 (The Nile Basin)

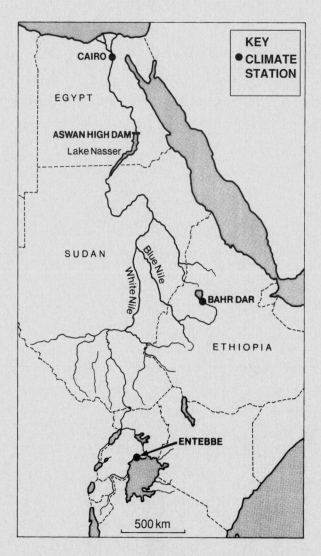

Question 3 – continued

Reference Diagram Q3A (Selected climate graphs)

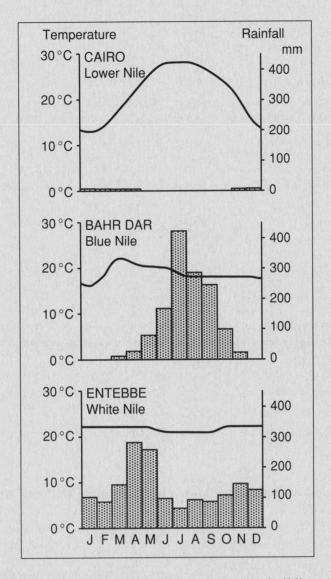

Reference Diagram Q3B (River Nile discharge before and after the building of the Aswan High Dam)

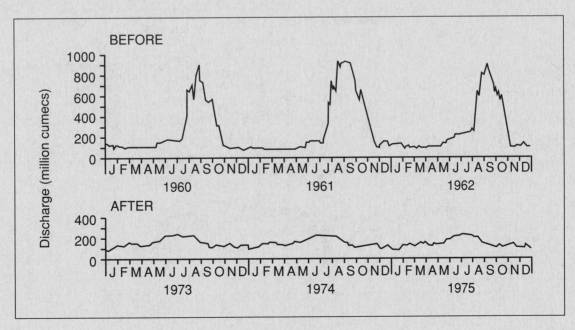

Marks

SECTION 2

You must answer ONE question from this Section.

Question 4 (Urban Change and its Management)

(a)   (i)   Study Reference Map Q4A.

With reference to the USA, **or** any other named country you have studied in the **Developed** World, **describe** and **explain** the distribution of major cities.   **5**

(ii)   Study Reference Map Q4B.

With reference to New York, **or** any named city you have studied in the **Developed** World, **describe** and **explain** the physical and human factors involved in its growth.   **5**

(iii)   In the second half of the 20th century, cities in the **Developed** World have undergone major changes in:

- housing
- industry
- shopping
- transport.

Choose **one** of the above and, for either New York **or** any named **Developed** World city you have studied, **describe** and **explain** the changes which have taken place.   **5**

(b)   Study Reference Diagram Q4.

Referring to Mexico City **or** a named city you have studied in the **Developing** World,

(i)   **describe** and **account** for its rapid growth, and

(ii)   **outline** the social and environmental problems which have resulted from this growth.   **10**

   (25)

Reference Map Q4A (Distribution of major cities in the USA)

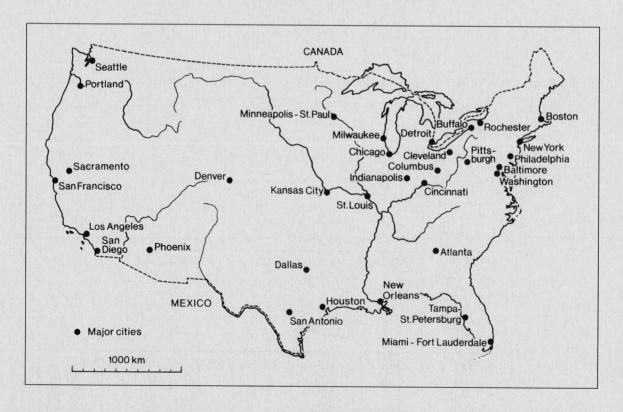

Question 4 – continued

Reference Map Q4B (The location of New York City)

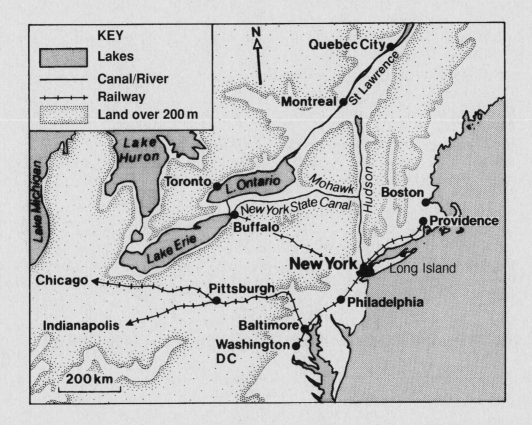

Reference Diagram Q4 (Population growth in Mexico City)

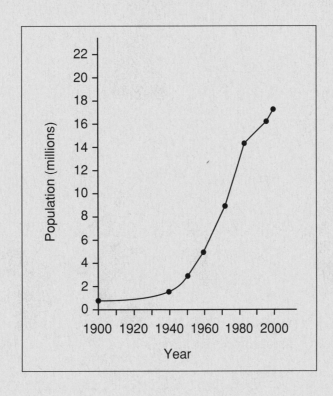

Marks

Question 5 (European Regional Inequalities)

(*a*) Study Reference Map Q5A which shows the areas which receive Objective 1 support. These areas are defined by the European Union as "lagging behind".

  (i) **Describe** the distribution of the areas classified by the European Union as "lagging behind".   **4**

  (ii) **Describe** the benefits which an Objective 1 area might receive from the European Union to assist in its development.   **4**

(*b*) Study Reference Map Q5B and Reference Table Q5.

"*Many European countries suffer from regional inequalities.*"

To what extent does the information shown illustrate the existence of regional inequalities in France?   **6**

(*c*) For any **named** country you have studied in the European Union,

  (i) **describe** the human and physical factors which have contributed to the development of regional inequalities, and   **7**

  (ii) **describe** the steps taken by the national government to reduce these inequalities, and comment on their effectiveness.   **4**

         (25)

Reference Map Q5A (Regions of the EU receiving Objective 1 funding, 1998)

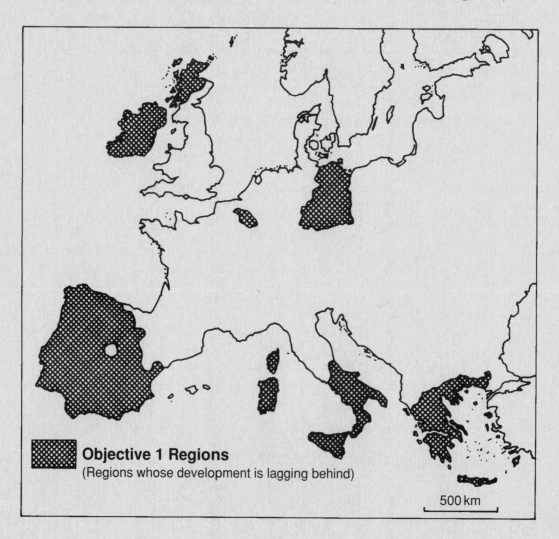

Objective 1 Regions
(Regions whose development is lagging behind)

500 km

Question 5 – continued

Reference Map Q5B (Regions of France)

Reference Table Q5 (Selected socio-economic data for Regions of France)

Region	Population Density (per sq km)	Migration Rate per thousand	GDP per capita (ECU)	Unemployment (percentage)
Nord/Pas de Calais	320·5	−2·7	91	16·3
Ile de France (includes Paris)	904·2	−0·8	173	10·9
Paris Basin	71·2	0·7	105	13·3
East	105·1	−2·4	106	9·7
West	88·6	4·0	95	11·6
South West	58·1	4·0	99	12·3
Centre-East	97·2	1·5	109	11·4
Mediterranean	100·5	5·5	98	15·9

Marks

Question 6 (Development and Health)

(a) Study Reference Table Q6.

The table shows that there are considerable differences in levels of development between countries in the **Developing** World. Referring to these countries and/or others in the Developing World which you have studied, **suggest reasons** why such differences **between** countries exist.

6

(b) Study Reference Diagram Q6.

With reference to countries of the Developing World with which you are familiar, **describe** and **suggest reasons** for the differences in the provision of social services between urban and rural areas.

5

(c) Primary Health Care strategies have been introduced by many countries in the Developing World in an effort to improve the health of the population.

Give examples of Primary Health Care strategies and **comment** on their effectiveness in improving health and controlling disease in areas you have studied.

6

(d) With reference to malaria **or** another water-related disease, **describe** the measures used to control the disease.

8

(25)

Reference Table Q6 (Indicators of development for selected countries)

Indicator	Saudi Arabia	South Korea	Ethiopia
GNP per capita (US dollars)	6910	8600	100
Life expectancy (years)	70	74	46
Infant mortality rate (per 1000 live births)	46	11	116
Birth rate (per 1000)	35	14	45

Reference Diagram Q6 (Access to social services in the Developing World)

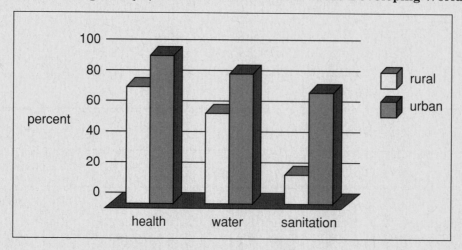

[END OF QUESTION PAPER]

[BLANK PAGE]

[BLANK PAGE]